SUCCESSFUL SELLING
FROM A TO $

John W. Rice has been a professional salesman and sales manager since 1947. A former vice president of a sales division at Houdaille Industries, Inc., a diversified Fortune 500 company, Mr. Rice has experimented with many diverse techniques and methods of sales. He has garnered extensive experience in training and developing sales personnel, as well as in writing training and catalog materials.

JOHN W. RICE

SUCCESSFUL SELLING FROM A TO

THE PROFESSIONAL'S GUIDE TO MONEY-MAKING SALES TECHNIQUES

A SPECTRUM BOOK

Prentice-Hall, Inc., Englewood Cliffs, New Jersey 07632

Library of Congress Cataloging in Publication Data

Rice, John W.
 Successful selling from A to $.

 "A Spectrum Book."
 Includes index.
 1. Selling. I. Title.
HF5438.25.R5   1983   658.8'5   82-20455
ISBN 0-13-872069-X
ISBN 0-13-872051-7 (pbk.)

This book is available at a special discount when ordered in
bulk quantities. Contact Prentice-Hall, Inc., General
Publishing Division, Special Sales, Englewood Cliffs, N.J. 07632

10 9 8 7 6 5 4 3 2 1

ISBN 0-13-872069-X

ISBN 0-13-872051-7 {PBK.}

Editorial/production supervision by Kimberly Mazur
Cover design by Hal Siegel
Manufacturing buyer: Pat Mahoney

Prentice-Hall International, Inc., London
Prentice-Hall of Australia Pty. Limited, Sydney
Prentice-Hall Canada Inc., Toronto
Prentice-Hall of India Private Limited, New Delhi
Prentice-Hall of Japan, Inc., Tokyo
Prentice-Hall of Southeast Asia Pte. Ltd., Singapore
Whitehall Books Limited, Wellington, New Zealand
Editora Prentice-Hall do Brasil Ltda., Rio de Janeiro

To my family,
who has made it all worthwhile

Contents

Foreword

This text belongs among the personal "how-to" books of every sales-person. For the young aspirant of a sales career, Mr. Rice describes specific sales situations that are encountered by the sales professional. His educated insight into the motives of personnel responsible for buying is ample justification for the time spent in reading this book. His practical advice in managing selling situations can give the equivalent of years of experience to a newcomer in the sales profession.

For the seasoned veteran, the text serves as a "try this" approach to circumstances of sales resistance. Likewise, for the purchasing agent, engineer, or manager involved in the buying process, the book describes the subtleties of the buy-sell relationship and provides a mirror reflection of how actions of the buyer are perceived by the sales person.

In the latter chapters, the author provides his personal philosophy on those characteristics of successful business people. Whether the reader is the "traditional manager" or what some have termed as the "new breed," a personal inventory of these characteristics will be beneficial.

A real student of the selling profession, Mr. Rice has 35 years of practical experience that makes this book uniquely different from those

written by the theorists. He goes beyond the definition of the problem—
he recommends solutions.

Mr. Rice spent his career as a practicing sales professional and from
his experiences, gained both in field sales and sales management, he provides the reader with the perspective of the successful salesman from the
bottom up and the top down. He has "practiced what he preaches," and
it has worked.

J. A. Johns

Preface

If you make your living in sales, how well you do is up to you to a larger extent than it might be in most other fields.

WHAT, FOR WHOM, AND WHY

This book is an educational aid for all who are involved with sales, regardless of their previous training or their experience level, regardless of the products or services they sell or to whom, whether they work inside or out, and whether they are actually on the line selling day after day or working in some capacity of sales management.

The primary objective is to cover all of the basic needs in one volume and to discuss them in detail sufficient to enable the reader to develop and refine, on his or her own if necessary, the skills needed to increase sales immediately.

More specifically, my purpose is to suggest practices and techniques (that I know have worked) to enable the reader to reach the goal of professionalism no matter how ambitious it is—and to do that with much less frustration and wasted time than gaining the necessary knowledge through thirty or more years of experience.

THE NEED

Selling, as much as any profession, offers unique challenges, but those are compensated by equally extraordinary opportunities. Both the challenges and the opportunities embrace special needs:

1. *To a great extent, salespersons must train themselves.* Regardless of the formal programs and the training literature with which they are constantly bombarded, there is still much they can and must do *on their own* if they are to develop the expertise that will clearly mark them as professionals in their chosen careers.

2. *The need for self-improvement is continuing.* Study by salespersons must go on and on with all of the aids available to them. They must be observant for the new lesson or the refinement of an old one that nearly every sales exposure affords an observant student of selling.

3. *We all need help.* All of us must admit one thing even though we are reluctant to do so—no matter how willing and eager we are, none of us is as effective as we could be if we used all of our capabilities most of the time. In many situations we flounder trying to figure out what to do, we make many mistakes by not thinking, and we fail to learn from the most obvious daily lessons.

I know all about that from experience, but I was fortunate enough to meet a couple of excellent teachers and read some excellent books early in my career. They showed me what selling is all about and what success demands.

4. *Selling is selling is selling.* There are innumerable classifications of selling, based on the class or type of product involved, the clientele or industry, the activity required, and many other criteria. But in all of them, no matter how diverse they are in some respects, there is one conspicuous similarity—many of the elements required for success are common to all. The analysis of the need is the same; the determination of the solution employs the same logic; the planning and preparation are similar; and for the execution of the plan to close the sale, the same techniques are effective.

5. *Selling is a new ball game today.* Many of us used to think, and maybe some self-deluded souls still do, that selling is little more than a glad-handing, politicking, back-slapping, arm-twisting effort to sell something to somebody whether he or she needs or wants it or not. And maybe the old tactics are still good for a score once in a while. But once in a while is no longer often enough.

Today, selling is a serious and demanding profession, but that very feature is one of its most desirable. That means that anybody who wants to study and work at it diligently can build a successful career in sales and reap the rewards the profession offers.

THE APPENDICES

Two appendices are included to present extra details on a couple of subjects, which would have disrupted the flow if they had been included in the basic text.

One of those relates to the procedure for planning the coverage of a sales territory. This is the most important plan of all and the cornerstone for all other planning.

For that basic planning there are two procedures. You can study your potential in a general way and allocate your time and your calls based on the judgment your study suggests. Or you can meticulously assemble and analyze all prospective sales dollars, estimate the time you have for each of those dollars of sales potential, and assign your time according to the resultant proportion.

Both methods are presented to you—the more general, less precise, quicker method in the basic text and the more detailed, more thorough one in the appendix. In the territories for which I had to plan the coverage, I used the more elaborate method and I found that the extra effort showed me more quickly and more precisely where I should be devoting my time.

MY APOLOGIES—

First, for the personal, subjective note ... It is difficult to cite personal experiences without sounding conceited, but I could not expect to make statements that you could accept unless I were able to support them with firsthand, personal knowledge. Nor would you want those supporting experiences to be anything less than stories of accomplishment.

But I made mistakes, too—so many that I hate to think of them except for the fact that I learned as much from most of them as I did from the successes.

Second, for repetition at times ...

The repetition is intentional because selling and teaching require repetition. A sales message or a lesson that is not repeated again and again even to the same listener is soon forgotten.

THE CHALLENGE

The last chapter might sound like holier-than-thou preaching to an errant, young convert. It is not intended to be that and I would be remiss if, after so much time for learning (again from the mistakes I made to a large extent), I did not try to pass on to anyone who would listen some of the lessons that cost me so much.

That last chapter really contains the challenge for all aspiring sales professionals.

Each of us has an amazing opportunity. We can set goals that we can define and clearly delineate with an actual model. We can select several individuals and build that model from the most desirable traits and strengths of each. Then we can keep that model before us and emulate it as we strive to reach our goals.

There is no better arena for one fired with ambition to reach clearly defined goals than in sales. For anyone who will expend the effort to become a professional salesperson there is a most challenging, lucrative, and satisfying career.

I wish I could start mine all over again. As I think about it, maybe that is just what I am doing as I begin this.

ACKNOWLEDGMENTS

I am indebted to my wife who, in addition to her ever-present support, helped greatly in reading the manuscript and suggesting improvements.

I am also grateful to Jack A. Johns, one of the most capable managers I have been privileged to know, for reading the manuscript, for making several suggestions, and for writing the *Foreword*.

part one

ANALYZING
AND
SATISFYING
THE SALES NEEDS

chapter one

Introduction

*Selling is a profession and it is vital to our national productivity
as measured by our Gross National Product.*

GROSS NATIONAL PRODUCT

In 1980, the Gross National Product (GNP—all goods and services produced in the United States valued at market prices) exceeded $2,626 billion based on the value of the dollar at the time.

In the numbers system this would be trillions of dollars, but trillion is not a very clear denomination. It is so big that it hampers easy comprehension. There is another problem, too. All nations are not in accord on the definition of a trillion and the crazy result is that its very magnitude differs immensely. For example, in France and the United States, one even trillion is the numeral *1* followed by twelve zeros; in England, the same trillion is the numeral *1* followed by eighteen zeros.

As you can readily imagine, quite a misunderstanding could result among unsuspecting citizens of France or the United States and Great Britain. In any event, the GNP for the United States in 1980 was more than $2,626,000,000,000 according to the French and United States understanding of trillion, and that is a lot of dollars no matter how expressed.

SELLING AND THE GNP

How does GNP relate to sales? That figure of $2,626 billion has a suggestion of the total number of dollars worth of goods and services sold in 1980, because if there is one pivotal function in getting all of those goods and services to the ultimate user, that function has to be sales. As a matter of fact, if it were not for the professional salespeople, the GNP would decline significantly. Without someone to apply and sell the products and services offered, fewer and fewer would be sold and the market, and the GNP, would diminish accordingly.

The arena for the sales responsibility is squarely in the middle of that GNP and no other function in the cycle has been more vital to its growth.

ABOUT SELLING

Selling is a profession just as surely as any other. One must be called to make it his or her chosen career and after that, must learn about it and then think about how to apply that knowledge. All of that requires skill that must be developed. Salespersons cannot approach their jobs as they would manual labor in which they need only to report to work and do the best they can with their physical and mental capabilities on any assigned task.

There is an old cliché that nothing happens until somebody sells something. It is an attention-getting opener for a sales meeting and I have used it many times.

In an important sense the statement is true. Little can be accomplished before that first sale. Nothing can be gained by the salesperson and, even more vital, the supplier represented can make no progress toward satisfying the reason to be in business. No money can be returned against the company's tremendous investment.

In another sense, much must happen before a sale can be made. For most products inventories must be built up to fill the entire supply system. Some products will just not sell unless they are immediately available. And very few will sell themselves. The sales organization must be assembled, trained, provided with the necessary sales tools, and put in place.

Indeed, there is a lesson in the old cliché for all salespersons, but they should not be totally misled by the suggestion that nothing happens before a sale is made. Perhaps, for some sales personnel nothing really does happen before a sale, but they would be the ones who plod through a sales career thinking that nothing much happens anyway. For the serious aspirant to sales success, much must happen. Most of them accept that and do something before they expect an order. Their only problem is that they do not always do what could be most effective for them.

It behooves salespersons to know what it is that they can do on a continuing basis to help themselves. One of these actions that has been given the least attention is the planning of the sales strategy and tactics based on a thorough analysis of the requirements of all possible sales situations.

Much has been written about techniques for arousing interest, presenting the sales story, special methods for closing the sale, and a host of other facets of supersalesmanship. And manufacturers have told their people about the products to the point of boredom. But few have done much or said much to help their salespeople plan the day-to-day work to gain the most sales from the time available to them.

In a way, the most effective sales effort evolves into a complete discipline. It means reducing each sales opportunity or each problem to a four-step course to a successful completion:

1. Critical analysis of the need or the problem.
2. Determination of the solution.
3. Preparation and planning.
4. Execution of the plan.

THE RESPONSIBILITIES OF SELLING

It is incumbent upon all salespersons to do their best because they carry a very great responsibility as professionals. That should be most evident to them as they reflect on their personal contributions to the staggering magnitude of the GNP. They share responsibility not only for the plateau it reaches but also for its composition. To a large extent, how well they do and in what direction they employ their talents determine a lot about how much our GNP is and how beneficial are its elements.

That is an important and awesome assignment.

BE A PRO

Accept the fact that selling requires the development and refinement of a skill for the attainment of professional status. Then go to work and become a pro.

chapter two

Buyers and buying motives

What could be a more appropriate and logical start for a discussion of sales than an analysis of buyers and what motivates them?

WHO THE BUYERS ARE

Buyers cover a wide range. On one end is a lone individual buying for himself or herself as a consumer in the so-called retail field. He or she decides what is needed or wanted and gets it if the money or the credit is available.

The other end of the range relates to the purchasing function of an industrial company or other entity. Even within this group, the persons involved in a purchase decision can vary greatly. A lone buyer or clerk might decide on routine requirements of small cost, but when a new machine or a new system for processing, or a really large purchase of any sort are involved, a dozen or more persons might be employed in the final buying decision. Among them may be several persons outside the purchasing department.

NEED OR DESIRE

Two things actually trigger most purchases—need or desire. In the retail field need is a most important factor, but desire also prompts a lot of purchasing by the consuming public.

A man sees a pretty golf shirt and wants it because it will go well with the slacks he bought last week. Or a woman is going to a special party and has to have a new dress, a new bag, and the endless accessories that make up a new outfit.

In the industrial field there is not much reason to buy other than need. The need might not be critical, but it must exist. It can take varied forms and have different degrees, from an immediate replacement for a broken part on a machine that is temporarily out of production to a need for a new system to reduce costs, improve quality, increase production, or accomplish all three.

There is for industrial buyers another requirement coupled with the need. At some point, most needs reduce to money. If an expenditure cannot save money, it can be difficult to justify. The final decision about purchasing, other than in emergencies, is tied to the bottom line of the financial statements.

Even what might seem like a desire for an industrial purchase is actually more an obscure need than the apparent desire. For example, consider an office expansion and renovation by a company that already has adequate facilities. Such an expenditure is not normally considered merely because the person with the ultimate authority desires a new office. What more likely inspires the decision is a belief that better working conditions will be more conducive to greater efficiency. The new office could also have much benefit in presenting a better company image and lead indirectly to increased sales. There is actually a need.

GENERAL BUYING MOTIVES

While the many who can be involved in industrial purchasing share a common purpose, they have different buying motives and each will require special sales treatment. This means that all buyers and all buying motives must be considered by the salesperson in preparation for any situation that might arise.

For industrial buyers, all motives can probably be classified into three broad categories (listed in order of consideration):

1. Motives based on the character and policies of the company.
2. Motives inspired by the individual's idiosyncracies and personality traits.
3. Motives related to the positions and responsibilities of the employees.

Motives Related to the Company

All companies have character. The nature of that character is sometimes difficult to appraise, but it is probably what determines the company's image—that new quality understood and so often discussed in today's sophisticated business climate.

First thoughts about image are that it develops and shines principally for outsiders and primarily for those who are customers or prospects. For example, many companies are regarded generally as class organizations by all of their customers and potential buyers. They manufacture a quality line of products, provide excellent service, quibble little about justified complaints, employ only high-caliber people, train them to be considerate and accommodating, and generally do things that make it pleasant and rewarding to do business with them.

But that image does not necessarily reflect only outwardly. The same things that determine the outward image also define for employees the total character of the company. That character is manifested in the general buying policies and motives. Some companies want only the best, just as they assume that their customers do when they give those customers the best quality they can. These companies do not quibble over prices once they have been accepted as fair, and their purchasing practices are considerate and ethical. These companies are just as good to sell to as they are to buy from.

On the other hand, there are companies that are less highly regarded by their general clientele. The quality of their products is not always in the Cadillac class; their policies are seldom the most sympathetic to customers; and even their purchasing habits are less than admirable.

As a matter of fact, there are entire industries in which most of the companies are similar to the latter description. It may be unfair to classify them in that manner, because the very competitive nature of the industry might mandate that they never relax their digging and scratching just to survive. It would not be fair or tactful to mention examples of such companies or industries, but their existence must be recognized and considered. Salespersons must take special note of how the caliber of various companies can affect their buying motives.

The one who can adapt his or her sales efforts to changing requirements is well on the way to becoming a professional and to gaining professional results.

Motives Related to the Individual

The most complex of all buying motives are embraced in the psychological traits of individual consumers. No two are the same and the range of classifications they inspire is well known to most people—all the way from introvert to extrovert, with myriad gradations between the extremes.

Nor is any one individual consistent. The condition of one's ulcer on a given day can profoundly affect his or her mood and willingness to buy, as can his or her spouse's temper or mood, or numerous other small incidents. Throughout our lives we have been told and have seen that simple experiences can cause significant changes of mood—even to the point of deserting our warm beds from the wrong side in the morning.

You know that people are like that. It has been illustrated to you time and again. Just think of a day when you were in an especially jovial mood and slapped your always cordial friend Joe on the back with a vigor inspired by your good spirits. And remember your utter shock when Joe exploded with a temper tantrum.

You were amazed to the point that you could not even react for a few seconds. Joe had never before given the impression that he was like that—not old, steady Joe. Later a friend who had witnessed the scene offered his explanation: "Don't think anything of it. Joe has a real problem with that son of his and it's about to get him down."

The explanation was immediately believable. You know people are like that.

Obviously, a salesperson cannot be an expert in all phases of human psychology, but he or she must strive to anticipate the shades of temper of the prospects encountered. That is what makes selling a thinking person's job and a challenge.

Motives Related to Positions

Motives related to the positions and responsibilities of the employees are the least subtle. They derive from the job specifications of each position. A purchasing agent has interests uniquely related to his or her job; a department head has different ones, and so on for the other employees who influence purchases.

Remember This

The principal reasons for buying are need and desire.

In the industrial field, it is primarily need.

Buying motives are influenced by the buyer's personality, the character of the company, and his or her position in that company.

Consider these factors as you prepare and execute your sales plan.

SPECIFIC BUYING MOTIVES

(Note: As specific buying motives are discussed, special sales considerations will be called to your attention. These are not all of the sales factors for any given instance but only a reminder of those that are peculiar and important to the position. Other sections will cover all facets of the sales requirements.)

Purchasing

Purchasing personnel have to be considered first. Regardless of their role or the authority they command, they are designated as being responsible for purchases and are the clearing point for them. Sales calls usually start with the purchasing department.

That department can range from one employee on a part-time basis to a major division of the company, employing a corps of buyers and senior buyers, and headed by a corporate officer such as director of purchases, who might be as aloof and unapproachable as the chief executive officer.

Whatever the title is, anyone in purchasing is buying for the company, spending company money, and has special reasons and objections for all decisions. The first is to save the company money. That is the job of purchasing people and they are reminded of that almost daily. They are rated by their superiors on how well they do that.

All of the buyers have equally important motives that are more personal. They want to buy correct parts or materials. If they buy something for a department head that does not perform the services necessary, everything that goes wrong in that department will be blamed on that purchase. On the other hand, if a buyer can obtain something that will help a department head, that department head will be a booster for the buyer—at least for a few days.

A secondary concern of all of the buyers is the filling of the orders after they have been placed. Buyers want delivery of exactly what they ordered and ON TIME. For them, expediting delivery is not directly productive. The buyers would prefer to devote their time to more positive action than solving problems.

Even more unpleasant than the wasted time and energy is the flack the buyer gets if a critically needed item is behind the promised delivery schedule. When that happens, even the grateful department head for whom the buyer has just done a great service deserts him or her. The department head has no compunction about complaining at the weekly or monthly meetings held for the review of the status of all open P.O.'s. Those meetings can be very uncomfortable for buyers who, in their turn, have very unkind thoughts about the salespeople of the offending company.

Beyond the normal desires and requirements, all buyers will have others about which they are especially sensitive and demanding. As a salesperson, you must find out what those are for each individual and satisfy them.

Special Sales Considerations

You will probably not have the good fortune to always be able to offer the lowest price. It is better to not always be low, but to always have the ammunition to combat low price competition and to know how to use it.

When you suspect or learn that your price is higher than a competitor's, find some other way to present the real cost. Show the buyer the greater value of your product—its better production capability, longer expected life, less maintenance, greater safety, or whatever you can imagine will convince that buyer that your product is the best buy in the long run. Even if you are competitive, such advantages should be stressed.

You can also help the buyer whose primary concern is satisfying a department head who intimidates him or her. Suggest that you might help convince the department head and offer to go see whoever that person might be. Point out to the buyer that you can help absorb the responsibility for the purchase.

After you have an order, make certain that it is handled to satisfy the customer completely. Make a special effort to do this on the first sale, not to mislead a new customer about your service unfairly, but because you must build some success with him for future orders. You will learn how important this post-sales service is the first time a buyer tells you, "We are giving you this order because of your past performance."

Engineering

Engineers are the technical people. They have many of the same personal desires and anxieties as the buyers. They, too, want to discharge their responsibilities to gain themselves job satisfaction, recognition, and opportunity, but their emphasis is different.

Price is important to them in only a general way; they feel obligated to place more emphasis on other factors. Their primary interest is in how the material, part, or machine will perform. Will it work? How does it show that? How is it made or built? What features will ensure that it will work and that it will last? How can it make their jobs easier? Can it increase production? How will it affect the costs of the product? What kind of maintenance is required and how much? Can it contribute to better quality? Does it fit into future plans?

Most engineers are also interested in the basic design and overall appearance when a machine or a system is involved. The design and engineering must be in accordance with good practice and must indicate that the machine or system will do the job. Once that has been established, there is an esthetic consideration. A flawlessly designed machine or a perfectly machined part is as inspiring to an engineer as a beautiful work of art is to a connoisseur of fine artistic creations.

This last consideration is more important than you might think. You might feel, as I have, that appearances should not be that critical. If it works, what is the difference how it looks? After all, no factory is supposed to double as an art gallery. I learned that engineers do not always agree on that.

One day several of us were meeting to discuss a processing machine that our chief engineer had designed. A particular feature was mentioned that seemed to have more to do with appearance than utility. It drew an immediate response from the CEO, "Aw hell, we don't need that. You all know that Jake wants to gold plate everything."

Of course, there is much logic in the engineer's approach. The more attractive the design is, the more likely it is to be a good machine. No engineer wants his or her name on a creation that looks like a mechanical abnormality. If such a machine fails, the engineer will be severely criticized again and again.

Special Sales Considerations

Salespersons need to speak the language of engineers; they need to emphasize the design and production features that answer the engineers' questions.

Long-range cost benefits should be emphasized over the initial price. The engineer wants to be sure that the equipment will produce, that it will last, and that in the end it will contribute most to quality, efficiency, and economy, even if it initially costs a little more.

For the salesperson who is not an engineer, the best source of information in compiling a sales plan for engineers is his or her own engineering department. He or she should talk to them and get some ideas about their point of view on the product's sales features.

Maintenance

The influence of the maintenance personnel in most companies might not be as great as that of other personnel. Maintenance is in some ways a subordinate department. It is strictly nonproductive overhead and most plant managers would be delighted if there were no need for maintenance or repair work other than changing a small light bulb—even then not too often and not too high off the floor.

But it is a necessary department and its activities are normally supervised very carefully. That is especially true when the big board shows a lot of machines "down" (out of operation for repair or rework). That big board just about manages the daily life of the maintenance crew.

Most plants have such a board, and it can be elaborate. All of the major machines are listed by number, type, model, and size, or by some other designation that clearly identifies the machine. Then on each line listing a machine, there are holes, slots, or lights to denote the status of various maintenance requirements.

There is always a special light or peg to indicate when a machine is down. When there are just a few machines down, those lights dominate the board no matter how many other machines listed show no problems. And the big board, often eight to ten feet across and four to six feet high, dominates the entire plant when it is well lit up with "down" lights. After a long absence from the office I used to make the big board my first check when I returned. By the number of lights, I could anticipate the mood to expect when all of the others came in.

It is funny about those boards. The designations that are given to the machines seem to eventually endow each one with its own character. Anything mechanical has a potential to break down, and in the case of machines, there are some which apparently have this tendency to a greater degree than others, regardless of their age, the use to which they have been subjected, or the operators who have run them. That is where the maintenance personnel come in and I think that some of them frequently wish that they could change the labels of some machines in an effort to change the characters, performance, and reliability of those machines.

The interest of the maintenance people is specific, and the more lights showing "down," the more specific it is. Their specific objective is to keep everything running and to make sure that any emergency that does occur happens during the daytime and not when they have to be called out of a warm bed. Those calls are funny, too. They never come fifteen or twenty minutes before the alarm is due to ring but only when there are still hours of good sleeping left.

Most companies wisely involve their maintenance department personnel in decisions about most large machinery expenditures. They need opinions based on experience and, equally important, they want to make maintenance department personnel feel they were a part of the buy decision. That can forestall a lot of complaints when some expensive unit starts breaking down regularly before the final installment on its purchase has been paid. Oddly enough, too, a maintenance person will have much less difficulty repairing a machine that he or she recommended be purchased.

Special Sales Considerations

A salesperson can help his or her case with the maintenance people by showing them how trouble free the machine is. They like to hear about others who use one with a minimum of lost time. They like to know that preventive maintenance programs are effective and easy to conduct.

They are vitally interested in the difficulty of repair when it does become necessary, and they want to know where they can get parts and what service organization is available to help them.

These people deserve your attention because theirs is a difficult and thankless job. They can become good support for future purchases and they will make excellent references for you to use with other prospects. And, best of all, they might be the easiest of all departments to work with.

Finance

Financial people think that they assume responsibility for which no one else in the entire organization has much sympathy. They often believe that the bottom line is up to them alone and that no one else seems to care—not even the chief executive officer (CEO) on some occasions.

When expenses mount and sales and profits fall, they are the first to be called for an explanation, and the questions are sharp and penetrating. What happened? Where did our profits go? Can't you control costs? Didn't you see this coming? Why didn't we know about it? What can we do?

After repeated sessions focusing on those questions, financial personnel sometimes come to feel that all of the unexpected misfortune was caused by some dereliction on their part. And that feeling is aggravated by the fact that every suggestion they make is thought to be irrelevant or biased and is opposed by every department head.

When there is no short-profit crisis occupying their full attention, their interests relate to the soundness of the investment from the standpoint of expenditure and the return to be expected. They ask themselves, can we afford it? How long will it take to recoup the cost?

They tend to disqualify themselves from any technical considerations, and they are the last to indulge in the aesthetic appreciation of the engineers. With such interests, financial people can sometimes be convinced that the least expensive option is not always the most economical.

Special Sales Considerations

Sales contact is not always made directly with the financial departments. As a result, the money considerations must be stressed with others to make sure that they are given full consideration and that all questions of the controller and his or her crew are answered. The purchasing department and CEO are two spots where the economy features should be emphasized.

If there is a general meeting for a final presentation, financial personnel are apt to be present. This suggests that all aspects of any possible savings should be fully explained during this meeting for the special benefit of financial personnel.

Safety

The safety department is to some degree subordinate like the maintenance department, but it receives lots of attention these days. Its performance is often publicized in a way that all who enter the plant can see. At many plant entrances, a big sign tells exactly how many days have passed since the last lost-time accident.

Often there is another sign in the plant that emphasizes safety. That one says, "Safety Is No Accident." Job injuries are the most devastating of all expenses and each lost-time accident is a compound expense. The expense of medical treatment is escalating daily, but equally costly is the lost time of the injured employee who is trained to fill a vital position in a manufacturing sequence.

And the expense does not stop there. Accident insurance is experience rated, which simply means that the more persons for whom injury claims are paid, the more the insurance rate increases. The final blow is the increase in the number of lawsuits involving serious bodily injury. More and more awards are made to the injured in today's courts.

There is little doubt about the interest safety personnel have in all new equipment purchases. To them, the best and least expensive machine in the world is worthless if it is booby-trapped for the operator.

The same considerations that interest the safety people have inspired top management to involve these personnel in more and more purchases of items that affect employee safety.

Special Sales Considerations

Salespersons should be aware of this interest because of the increased emphasis of their own engineers on the safety features of the equipment they sell. Nowadays even small power tools are literally covered with safety instructions. There is no mistaking the present emphasis on safety and there is no slackening of that emphasis in sight. Government regulations will ensure that.

The most important signal that this sends to the salesperson is to emphasize the safety features of the product. Since he or she does not always have the opportunity to talk to safety department personnel, this is another part of the story that must be told to others who will pass along the word.

Department Head

Along with personal desires, the department head has interests that are peculiar to the assignment as head of a department. The department head's overriding concern is his or her own little bailiwick.

What other departments do is not that important unless their mistakes affect others. As long as good parts keep flowing into any given department, the head of that department can achieve its purpose—to move them through at maximum speed with as few rejects as possible and at the lowest possible cost per part.

The department head is important in deciding about purchases of machinery for that department. All good department heads know best about the problems that can be encountered and most about machines of the type that will contribute most to the success of their departments.

In all departments there are supervisors and key production people who can materially help in evaluating the potential performance of a new machine. If they add their endorsements to a machine selection, the odds are that its production will be greatly aided. The reverse is certainly true for when department personnel do not like the selection they can make a fine choice look like a purchasing disaster.

Special Sales Considerations

Simplicity and ease of setup, a requirement for minimum maintenance, and safety are all important to production personnel, but their chief concerns involve production capability and ease of operation. They want parts, and they are competing with all other departments for output and costs.

It is difficult for salespersons to demonstrate machine operation in the department, but they must surely discuss the machine's capability in detail.

Production people are good prospects to invite to your plant, to a machine fair, to another customer's plant, or anywhere they might see in operation an actual machine of the type they propose to buy.

Chief Executive Officer

The CEO has personal desires and goals, too. He or she is considerably more ambitious than most of the others, and different persons will be rating his or her performance.

The CEO is not much concerned with the personal motives of the others. He or she wants their help in deciding what is best for the company, and expects good, sound advice in the area of each advisor's special expertise. The CEO must rely so much on the input of these others that in some cases his or her strength comes from knowing these people and evaluating their comments. The CEO will have areas of special expertise but, even then, a good manager will heed the advice of subordinates. The manager who does not is not taking full advantage of their skills.

By the time the CEO sees the salesperson, he or she has probably reduced all doubts to a few points and will be most anxious to clarify them quickly.

Another concern is important to the CEO. When the final decision is made, he or she wants as many employees as possible to be satisfied with it.

Special Sales Considerations

When finally granted a brief appointment with the CEO, the salesperson should immediately try to discern the CEO's points of chief interest. That is normally not difficult. The CEO will not be reticent in most cases.

When all of these have been covered, the salesperson should be prepared to review some of the sales points already made to others. Here are some suggestions for points to include:

1. Reemphasize the major advantages, principally those related to quality of output, quantity, unit cost, low maintenance, safety, and after-the-sale service.
2. Include any advantages not already covered adequately.
3. Speak to any objections you sense that the CEO might have, but avoid calling them objections.
4. Repeat the salient points you have already presented to any others whom you suspect were not convinced or not fully capable of presenting a strong case for you to the others.

You are the one, too, to help the CEO convince the others about the wisdom of selecting your equipment. That is what you should have been doing all of the time. Do that some more after you have learned where more effort is required.

You might see the CEO only once or twice. That strongly suggests that you prepare fully for those meetings, that you execute your very best efforts, and that you learn as much as you possibly can about what else to do.

The CEO's Staff

On many large purchases, the CEO's top staff will have great influence, and frequently the salespersons who are left in the running will be invited to make their final presentation to this group. All of those whom you have already met will probably be present and there may be a few others.

Even those whom you have met previously can react quite differently in this meeting, since all of the executives are present. The eager beavers will be more aggressive; the reserved ones, more reticent; and the questions might be different from what you anticipate.

There is also a totally new possibility. The inner politics of the company might come to the surface in all of its picayune, counterproductive aspects.

Special Sales Considerations

This is the big presentation and Chapter 4 is devoted to such an exercise. Some points deserve special emphasis and repetition at this point:

1. If there are strangers in the group, try to learn as quickly as possible their interests and their areas of authority. Ask about them before your meeting starts, if possible.

2. Sort out those with the real clout. The interplay in the meeting might reveal some surprise in this area, different from what you might have expected during your previous meetings. Be alert for that possibility.

3. Unexpected questions in an unexpected tone might come up. For example, someone who has been most sympathetic before and who might have seemed most sold on your product might be much more curt and abrasive.

There could be two reasons for that. This individual might be trying to impress, but more likely is seeking the approval of others on some major point on which you have already satisfied him or her. If that point later proves to have been incorrectly judged, he or she wants to be able to say to any who point an accusing finger, "You heard what the salesmen said in the meeting just as I did."

Be tolerant of such questions and treat them seriously.

4. Shun the politics. Make believe there is no such thing.

This presentation will be more formal and more structured than any you might have had previously. It is time to prepare most thoroughly, using all of the tools available. It is probably the first chance you have had to close the sale. DO IT.

BE A PRO

No two buyers are the same and they vary in their buying motives as much as they differ in any other respect. A real pro will do the extra things necessary to understand these differences. He or she will attack each major influence on the motives of the buyer and analyze them until they are thoroughly understood.

The differences inspired by company and position in the company will be simplest. The professional salesperson will contemplate them, observe their results in different situations, and reason them through.

He or she will devote more attention and effort to gain an insight into the more complex personal motives. He or she will observe people with curiosity and will study them constantly. People are a challenge to a sales pro who meets that challenge head-on.

The most ambitious will read all that can be found on cogent subjects, will study some psychology, and might even enroll in a course or two. He or she will probably read the all-time classic, *How to Win Friends and Influence People* by Dale Carnegie and will likely enroll in one of the courses that have developed from Carnegie's efforts.

The real pro will be eager to know what makes a buyer tick. Every exposure to a buyer will be considered a learning opportunity and a chance to broaden his or her experience.

And as the salesperson learns and gains experience, he or she will become more flexible in directing the sales effort to the motives indicated by the buyer who is encountered at any particular moment.

chapter three

The anatomy of an order

As a followup to an analysis of buyers and their motives, a detailed look at the procedures they employ should be next.

PURCHASING AND SELLING

There are two sides to an order—the purchasing and the selling.

Purchasing

One way to consider purchasing people and their policies and procedures is to dissect an order—to literally take it apart and examine it, piece by piece, from need to negotiation.

The complexity of the purchasing procedure and the number of persons who have significant input into the final buying decision vary considerably from one need to another. The principal influences are the frequency of the need, the technical aspects of the requirement, and the size of the expenditure.

Inexpensive, small items that are purchased on a regular, routine basis are usually handled by purchasing department buyers or department heads. As a matter of fact, many such items are purchased on a contract. Prices and terms, quantities, back-up inventories, lead time, and other relevant details are negotiated in advance and then the purchase and supply become fairly automatic.

On the other extreme, a large capital expenditure for complicated machinery can require different handling in all respects, and all of those who will be affected by the purchase will contribute input based on their needs and their knowledge. A number of suppliers will be considered and a number of bidders will be specified. The final decision will not rest with the purchasing department alone but will likely be a consensus of the opinions of all who have participated in the process.

Selling

Purchasers need to be concerned only with their needs, their procedures, and their motives, with little regard to how salespeople do their jobs except as it affects the purchasers themselves.

Salespersons cannot afford to pay attention only to their side of the transaction. It is important that they know and understand the total purchasing function—the entire treatment of a potential order from the first awareness of the need all the way to the formal purchase order—sold, shipped, and paid for. They should be as familiar with those aspects as they are with the motives of those who approve the purchase and place the order. How else can they plan the sales effort required to satisfy all purchasing requirements?

I have often thought that a sales trainee could profit significantly from a tour of duty in a purchasing function. I knew one who had such buying experience, but he also had some of the important qualifications for sales and an inclination to try. As soon as he had developed those inclinations, he became a very successful salesman.

The sales efforts for the different purchase requirements also vary. For the small routine purchases, a salesperson needs to get acquainted with the buyer, make the sales presentation, convince the buyer that he or she can best serve the buyer's needs, and ask for the order. If that proves sufficient, good service and adequate follow-up contact will normally keep a share of the business.

When a contract is in effect, the salesperson's responsibilities are clear. He or she must ensure that his or her company provides the goods and services promised and that the customers live up to their end of the bargain. With the help of the close relationship that usually results from contractual associations, the salesperson should try to increase sales as much as possible in order to take advantage of such a preferred position. The additional potential is often the justification to supply a buyer on a contract that usually includes a price concession.

Selling the contract initially demands a thorough and effective effort. That is especially true if the salesperson has not had the contract before. Winning the contract in the first place is like the sale of a big order for an unusual and expensive requirement.

The big order involving a machine or a system, or a contract for many parts over a period of time, or any large expenditure normally brings into play all of the purchasing considerations and participants.

It is the type of requirement that might take a fairly long time to sell. During that time several calls will be required by the salespeople, who will visit many of the purchasing and other personnel. The big order is the type in which the salesperson's knowledge of the purchasing activity will be most helpful because he or she must carefully devise an overall strategy and then thoroughly plan and prepare for each individual contact.

FORMAT

It is easiest to cover all possible considerations by discussing in detail the most demanding and complicated sales requirement imaginable. With that in mind, it will be the anatomy of the big order that will be dissected here.

As each anatomical part is considered, the special sales objectives pertaining to that aspect of the purchasing function will be included. The more general requirements for all sales calls and presentations will not be mentioned since they are covered in Chapter Four.

THE ANATOMICAL PARTS OF AN ORDER

That brings us to the viscera of the order's anatomy—the vital parts of a purchase and sale:

1. Identification of Need
2. Definition of Requirements
3. Location of Sources
4. Detail of the Need
5. Proof of Feasibility and Affordability
6. Tentative Approval of the Project
7. Review of Availability and Finalization of Specifications
8. Preparation and Dissemination of Inquiry
9. Evaluation of Bids
10. Determination of Supplier and Negotiation of Order.

Whether these are distinct and isolated steps in the purchase process is immaterial. They all have to be considered. That consideration may be just agreement of only two or more individuals on one small point or it may involve long study and discussion by several persons. The sequence might also vary from the normal development indicated.

The salesperson must prepare and execute a strategy to satisfy whatever is necessary.

1. Identification of Need

Except for breakdowns or other emergencies, industrial needs entailing large expenditures do not normally come up instantaneously with no warning. A businessman does not just wake up one morning and suddenly decide that today he is going to buy a half-million-dollar machine, even if he alone can make that decision. An expenditure such as that has been anticipated and discussed long before a serious intention or critical need to act. In a large company, there have undoubtedly been lots of discussion and tentative approval in a business plan or a capital equipment budget.

Even a major breakdown should not catch everyone off guard. That particular machine has broken down so many times that its doing so once more should not be totally unexpected.

A need can be accelerated or brought to the purchase stage by any one of several developments. The most ordinary is probably the fact that its time has come on that approved budget.

A revised schedule for introduction of a new product can move a need forward. And sometimes a creative salesperson can accelerate a need by presenting a new or improved machine or system. Economic developments can be factors and a host of other events can affect a need but, in any case, it must become acute before the purchasing process can be set into motion.

Special Sales Considerations

Even if a salesperson making the first call to a new company just happens to catch a purchasing agent looking for a machine exactly like he or she offers, that salesperson may not be welcomed with, "Boy, am I glad to see you! We're looking for a machine right now that you probably can supply." It is just not in the nature of a purchasing agent to react that way.

The chances are good that the purchasing agent will start shuffling papers with renewed vigor and greet the visitor with, "You've really caught me at a bad time. I don't need anything and can only give you a few minutes." And he or she punctuates the last statement with a furtive glance at the clock.

With encouragement like that, the salesperson can barely resist scrapping his or her plan for the call and all of the objectives so clearly outlined. That is the wrong thing to do. Rise to the challenge.

When you are caught like that, proceed exactly as you planned. Try your best to arouse the buyer's interest by showing something and explaining what it can do for him or her. Base your presentation on the assumption that the buyer does need something, until you have been thoroughly convinced otherwise. You should even assume that there are big projects in the planning stage because they usually are for successful, forward-thinking companies.

Avoid permitting the buyer's warning that he or she has little time to bother you or cause you to hurry your presentation. Give the buyer lots of opportunity to talk, but keep him or her on your subject. Buyers cannot complain when they are talking and they might tell you something important. They might even give you a clue about a pending need.

Make an effort to see others in the plant. Try for a plant tour with the explanation that the buyer need not take the time if someone else is available.

Ask for an order. Convince the buyer that you came there to sell something, not to visit. Take notes. Leave some provocative thought as you depart.

After the call, write to the buyer. Thank him or her for the time and courtesy. Emphasize some point you made during your visit and send an envelope stuffer of some kind that relates to that point.

Parting Thoughts—A digression is justified here to say something more about leaving the buyer with some provocative thought as you depart. A couple of specific aspects of selling prompt that suggestion: 1) Success in sales depends a lot on the repetition of the sales message; unless even the most obvious advantage is repeated often, it will register only briefly or not at all with a prospect; and 2) when you want to make a sale, you have the best chance if you can deliver your own message; if you have to depend on someone else to do that, you must plant a seed of what you want said.

During the consideration of a major purchase, that project is the subject of a lot of discussion by all of those who are involved with the decision to buy and from whom. Just a casual exchange at the water fountain can make a significant impression on one of those deciders. That means that it makes sense to have every member of the buyer's staff spreading your sales message. The best way to do that is to give one major thought to each one who might be giving input to the final decision.

Think of the idea as an exercise in subliminal suggestion, an ultra-modern technique that many think is very productive. Thinking of it in that light, challenge your imagination to invent the most powerful phrase you can for each of your potential messengers. Look at this device as just another means available to broadcast your product's advantages. And be encouraged by the truism that very big decisions are often influenced disproportionately by seemingly insignificant factors.

It is difficult to give samples of phrases that merit such an aura of magic because they need to be derived from the discussions with each individual and a consideration of his or her nature and role. Here are some possibilities to stimulate your own thinking:

"This machine is the one that the entire industry has been trying to copy."

"Our company has become the recognized expert on the very application you have."

"The problem you have has become our specialty."

"This machine has the best performance record in the industry—best output, cheapest unit cost."

Different thoughts should be given to each different individual, again based on his or her particular interest in the purchase. But that same thought should be repeated again and again to that individual until he or she thinks that it is really his or her own idea, until that individual feels it strongly enough to suggest it to others at every opportunity.

2. Definition of Requirements

Even though a need has been the subject for lots of discussion, it is not always clearly defined in the early stages. Different personnel have different ideas about what is actually required to solve the problem. Surprisingly, not all of those who are going to help decide what to buy know exactly what is available.

Special Sales Considerations

At this stage your objectives are pretty much as they were on the first call. Try to meet more people and to arouse some interest in all you meet.

Learn all you can about your prospect and keep trying to uncover a need. If you are fortunate enough to hear about a specific requirement, discuss the models of your machines that can fill the need and convince all whom you meet that you should be considered as a supplier.

Again, ask for an order—even a small maintenance item, anything to get you started. Take notes. Leave a parting thought with all of those you see. Follow up in all cases that offer an opportunity. Write some letters.

3. Location of Sources

As soon as the need is adequately detailed, the potential buyer will gather more specific data on those suppliers who can ostensibly satisfy the need. Those who satisfy the prospect's requirements will probably be asked to submit a budget bid for their further discussing and planning.

Special Sales Considerations

By this time you have met several people, in the best situation have seen the plant, and you have a specific project to work on.

In spite of a compulsion to treat a preliminary bid lightly, it should be given serious consideration. Some suppliers submit low bids based on the assumption that the final requirements will be quite different. They reason falsely that a low bid will get immediate attention and a good first impression for them. That reasoning is unsound and that becomes obvious if that low bid backfires on them when they come in high on their quotation for the final specifications.

On the other hand, it is unwise to add contingencies that might not arise. Some who are too high on the first proposal are sometimes dropped from consideration if there are a lot of initial bidders. There really is only one alternative. Make your bid as realistic, accurate, and fair as you can. That will tell you more when you learn the results; you will have another chance, anyway.

The first look at the specifications provides an excellent chance to study the project and to suggest any changes you consider beneficial. These changes should not only be incorporated in your bid with an explanation, but they should also be discussed in person on your next visit. Convince the prospect that you can compete on the exact specifications but that you have ideas for improving the equipment selection. Naturally, if your suggestions employ features only your equipment will afford, so much the better.

Ask for an order, as always. Take notes. Repeat your parting thoughts. Follow up.

4. Detail of the Need

The budget bids will help the purchaser evaluate the project in more concrete terms. From this point on, discussions about the actual equipment to be purchased and the suppliers to be seriously considered will be on a much firmer basis.

Questions will be specific and will require more detailed answers. The buyer will be seeking all of the clarifications needed to help him or her decide just what is needed.

Special Sales Considerations

The budget bid you submitted should be followed up very closely with as many of the purchasing personnel as possible. You need to know how you did on this first test—where you stand, who the competitors are, and where they stand.

Be sure that your product selection is your best choice and begin to narrow the options you offer. Pursue aggressively any recommendations for changes you made on the budget bid. Explain your reasoning thoroughly and clear away any doubt that might exist. If there are too many controversial reactions, withdraw your suggestions. If your advice is well received, begin a campaign to have your product, or major parts of it, specified on the final proposal. Try to make yours the benchmark for the "or equal."

If you have not yet met all who might possibly be involved in the buying decision, intensify your efforts to do that.

Ask for an order. Take notes; especially list your thoughts about what still needs emphasis and what will help you in your final presentation. Continue to leave those parting thoughts. Follow up with more letters to various persons you have met and make the letters more specific and detailed.

5. Proof of Feasibility and Affordability

Feasibility relates to the economic soundness of the expenditure. The project is feasible if it will make money or save money. It is nearly that simple.

This is one of the early critical tests. There have been many cases when this final feasibility study has caused a company to drop a complete process or even to eliminate part of the product line rather than approve an expenditure that did not appear to be viable. During the time when this is being written, there are violent shakedowns in many United States industries. Any one of the automobile companies could write a case history on this experience.

This is the time, too, when the home office shows heightened interest. They want hard numbers and they give them hard looks. Nothing about previous decisions remains sacred.

Affordability is closely related to feasibility. It, too, is fairly simple and embraces a couple of questions—is the money available? Or is it obtainable on a basis that will not destroy the feasibility? One sad fact is that if the money or acceptable credit are not available, the prospect of additional profit is academic. Chrysler Corporation learned all about that before the government bailed them out.

There is a little story that so exemplifies affordability that it has to be told. I heard this story just after World War II in Lancaster County, Pennsylvania, which was part of the first territory to which I was assigned. At the time, the county was one of the most agriculturally productive in the entire country and the principal reason for that ranking was the pre-dominance of the Amish people. They were known for their frugality and farming expertise.

As the story goes, one ambitious man and his wife wanted to buy the farm that adjoined theirs in just another step toward owning all they could get. At the closing of the transaction, the scene presented great contrast. The offices were posh and staffed with young Ivy Leaguers. Expensive briefcases lay all around. The buyers were plain, country folks (much to their credit) and they carried a couple of paper sacks. At the climax of the settlement, an exchange of money became necessary (as always). The amount was $26,000 and the man turned to his wife and said, "Give him the money, Mama."

Mama reached down and spilled the contents of one of the sacks on the fancy desk for counting. The money suddenly ran out just short of the needed $26,000 and Mama became very excited and embarrassed. The man remained cool as ever and with one terse statement solved the dilemma, "Looks like you just got the wrong sack, Mama."

That is affordability.

Special Sales Considerations

During this time of hard decisions, make sure that your prospect has all the cost-related data you can supply—machine performance records; letters of testimonials from satisfied customers; their cost economies, if they can be revealed; and anything else relating to the economies of operation of the equipment or use of the product.

If you have a lease plan or a lease-purchase agreement, make those details known. Stress any suggestions you have that make your proposal feasible and affordable.

If you have not been able to determine how you stand after the budget bid, continue your efforts on that. If you learn that you are competitive, stress that point only mildly at this point. You want to avoid the suggestion that price is your chief advantage and emphasize the superior quality of your product.

If you should discover that you are higher than your competitors, find out all you can about the difference. How high are you? In what respects are you high? Who are the lower bidders? You need all the information you can get if you are not competitive to guide your sales campaign and to prepare for the final quotation to come.

This would be a good time to invite some of their key people to visit your plant. Or bring some of yours to them. Enlist the help of other district personnel if the executive office is not in your district.

Ask for some kind of order. Take notes. Hammer in those departing thoughts. Follow up with letters or phone calls, or both. And one other suggestion—do not carry your money around in a paper sack these days.

6. Tentative Approval of the Project

This might seem out of place to you because you might have assumed that the project has already been approved. Until now, all approval has probably been conditional. No final OK has been given because there has not been enough concrete detail available. Costs have not been finalized and, undoubtedly, several other considerations are in the double-checking stage.

But the tentative approval is significant. It indicates that the basic tests have been passed. The approval is made tentative only to provide a hedge against some totally unexpected, adverse development.

Special Sales Considerations

You should now have a pretty good feel for where you stand and what you still need to accomplish. Confirm that as far as possible with your most responsive contacts.

Devote the necessary effort to any subjects that need more work and to any individuals not completely won over.

From this stage the purchasing process could proceed more rapidly. Check your strategy for the final thrust and prepare to intensify your efforts.

Ask for an order. Take notes. Repeat each parting shot. Follow up.

7. Review of Availability and Finalization of the Specifications

It might seem impossible to you that the prospect is still reviewing availability and deciding what he or she really wants.

It is like that in a great many of the cases entailing large expenditures. There is little room for error in such an important and costly project. In some cases, as many as six or eight quotation revisions are requested, seemingly with no compunction whatsoever by the prospect.

The review of availability really involves determination of which of the suppliers can furnish the most desirable product and if they can meet the delivery. It is merely a paring down of the final bidders list.

Based on all of the changes suggested by all suppliers, the final specifications have to be clarified and detailed to ensure that all will be quoting the same, "or equal."

Special Sales Considerations

You have two overriding objectives now: 1) make sure that your equipment is totally acceptable, and 2) ensure that you are on the final bidders list.

Most important, be patient and retain your enthusiasm. You might take a lot of time, too, if you were spending all of that money.

The engineers are deeply involved in this phase and all of your contacts should include them. Reduce all options to the minimum to eliminate confusion. Concentrate on the advantages of your final recommendations.

Make a maximum effort to have them incorporated in the specifications showing your part numbers.

Competition will begin to stiffen and every technique will be used, ethical and otherwise. Protect the dignity and image of your company by remaining aloof from the dirty tricks. And take heart—if all of your competitors are knocking you and your products, they obviously think that you present their biggest threat. If they say enough about you, the prospect will soon agree that you are.

Ask for an order. Takes notes. Leave your best parting shot. Follow up.

8. Preparation and Dissemination of Final Inquiry

The purchasing department now has to write the final details into the formal inquiry and send it to the bidders.

Special Sales Considerations

To complete your bid, your primary attention is devoted to your own people. Make sure that the application engineers understand the specifications and that they are in accord with all phases of them. Review all of your notes and go over them with the engineers and the estimators, stressing the competitive situation with them.

Then ensure that your proposal is prepared correctly. Be sure that it is complete with any notes or necessary explanations. Expand those as you need to in your letter of transmittal. Be certain the bid is mailed on time to meet the closing date.

If you think you can get an order by delivering the bid, call and arrange the necessary meeting or interviews. It is highly unlikely that the order will be placed before all bids have been analyzed and evaluated, so do not attempt the delivery unless you can be certain that the customer will order now.

Begin your preparation for any final presentation you might arrange.

9. Evaluation of Bids

When all of the bids have been received, the purchasing department evaluates them with the help of other departments as needed. This can be a complex job because all of the bid elements of the various suppliers are never precisely the same. It is sometimes tricky to compare the "or equal" as interpreted by some suppliers. Terms and conditions are expressed differently, and a common denominator must be devised to facilitate a consistent and objective comparison.

Normally on a large project with several bidders, a spread sheet is drawn up. The features of the proposals to be compared are shown across the top, and the competitors are listed down the side, or vice versa. The data for each supplier is added in the appropriate place to provide an overview of the relationship of each. Once the data are complete, the sheet is circulated or discussed with all concerned.

It could be very helpful for you to know about bid evaluation. A check of how your purchasing people do it could be educational and beneficial for you.

Special Sales Considerations
Your objective is utterly clear now—GET THE ORDER AS QUICKLY AS POSSIBLE after the bid review.

Call the prospect and ask for the order. Indicate that you expect it.

If you cannot get it, ask for an appointment to explain your bid and clarify all points with all who are concerned.

If you are told that the other bidders will be given the same opportunity, it probably means that no commitment will be made until all have had a chance to tell their stories. In that case, try your best to schedule your appointment last. You will then have an audience at the first instant that a decision is possible.

If you cannot get the order at this point, you have to learn all you can about the competitive situation. Contact all of the friends you have made during your long sales campaign and learn all you can about your status. If necessary, make a special trip to visit any of them before your meeting, if that appears beneficial.

10. Determination of Supplier and Negotiation of Order

The prospect is now ready to make the final supplier selection. The role of the purchasing department will probably be less important at this stage. Plant engineering, production, financial, department, and staff people will have the most influence over what happens now, guided by the analysis the purchasing department has made.

The chances are that all but two or three suppliers have been eliminated. The order could be issued with little further delay, or that final meeting could be scheduled with one or more of the surviving bidders.

It is also highly possible that the prospect could make an effort to negotiate a lower price now as well as during the final meeting. Some buyers hope to catch a supplier running scared and always try for a better deal. It is also a technique that is used if one of the acceptable bidders is to be eliminated unless that bidder's price can be reduced.

Special Sales Considerations
Make absolutely sure that you will have a scheduled time for that final meeting—last if possible.

If a price concession is mentioned at this time, tell the prospect that you will discuss that at the meeting.

Now prepare for the most important meeting of the entire sales campaign. Plan a full dress presentation as outlined in Chapter Four.

Perish the thought! But if you are told at any time during these final stages that you will not get the order, do not give up. Find out why you have lost and ask for one more meeting. If you have to, tell them that you know they are fair-minded and that they appreciate the work you have done and the recommendations that you made. Reiterate your conviction that you have the best product and that its price is right. You just want one more opportunity to make sure that you did not make a mistake in the bid and that it was clear in all respects when it was evaluated.

The two most common reasons for your loss would be a price disadvantage or an erroneous evaluation of your bid as compared with the others. You could be furnishing higher quality that is not readily discernible.

Based on these two possibilities and anything you can learn, prepare a presentation just as you would have for a final meeting as a surviving bidder, but consider more thoroughly all of the possible objections that could have prompted them to tell you that you would not get the order.

There is one more point to make if you get the order. It can best be introduced by a personal experience, but you should be cautioned that it is so nearly unbelievable that you might think it is a tale concocted to emphasize a point. I assure you that it happened.

Our men waged an intensive and well-planned sales campaign for an order for equipment to be used in a new sugar refinery to be built along the Mississippi River. The sale would have amounted to several hundred thousand dollars. The sugar company was a regular customer of ours at other plant locations, and they were using a lot of our equipment.

We were told that we had the order and that the formal contract would be in the mail in the next few days. After a couple of weeks there was still no order but there was a barely perceptible hint of the odor of that proverbial rat that someone is always smelling.

When we expressed more anxiety for the P.O. so that we could get the job into the schedule, we were told that there had been a change and the order had been given to a competitor. There is no need to mention that there was an immediate outbreak of sickness in our company.

Through our good friend in the sugar company we learned that the successful competitor had enlisted the help of the chief executive officer in the ivory tower in New York. That was not all that surprising because it was a good order. The real shocker was the sales argument that encouraged the change. It seems that the CEO of the supplier reminded the prospect that they had a plant right down the road from the site for the proposed sugar refinery and that it would not look too good to their mutual neighbors if they did not sell them the equipment.

At least that was the story we got from our reliable contact. Of course, a substantial price concession might have nourished that impulsive feeling of neighborliness.

But here is the point that should be made. When you get a commitment, wait for something in writing with a signature to authenticate it—a contract, a purchase order, a letter, or at least a general statement on a purchase-order form stipulating that details will follow.

Even among neighbors of the highest business echelons, something signed signifies that a deal has been made that cannot be changed without provocatlon.

BE A PRO

The professional salesperson will study purchasing as much as sales until he or she understands the total buying process, step by step.

Then that person can adapt the sales efforts to the requirements of each step.

chapter four

Sales presentations

Every business call should be considered an opportunity for a sales presentation, and the salesperson should be appropriately prepared to sell something.

The presentation is to sales what the weekend game is to an NFL football team. That is what it is all about—the reason for analyzing what it will take to win the next game, devising the game plan, preparing all week according to the plan, and then executing the plan to win or lose the objective in the game itself.

The anatomical metaphor is relevant here, too. There are distinct parts in a presentation and they are all related to each other in an orderly manner. To best understand the whole process, it is helpful to dissect each part, examine it closely, and study its correlation with the whole. So in a sense, this may be considered THE ANATOMY OF A PRESENTATION, just as an order was examined from an anatomical point of view.

THE PRESENTATION PARTS

These are the parts of a presentation:

1. Arouse interest.
2. Introduce your company.
3. Sell yourself.
4. Determine prospect's general needs.
5. Sell your product line.
6. Determine or create specific need.
7. Satisfy that need.
8. Complete the selling job.
9. Overcome objections; close sale.

1. Arouse Interest

This step of the presentation has a special importance. Unless the initial effort to arouse the prospect's interest is effective, the visit could be short and futile. There are several ways to create interest, but they all boil down to two: 1) what you say and how you say it, and 2) what you do and how you do it.

Continual attention is devoted to this element by both sales and advertising people who perennially strive to develop interest arousers. In fact, if the goal of advertising were simmered down to its quintessence, it would be to arouse the interest of all possible prospects even before the salesperson arrived.

To stimulate interest quickly and fully is the chief reason for many of the expensive and ingenious sales aids offered by most aggressive companies—samples, models, displays, brochures, films and film strips, slide series, and others.

The first suggestion to the salesperson, of course, is to use all of the sales aids that are available. They are expertly designed and meticulously produced, and they work! They work especially when the user is introducing a new product or addressing a new prospect. I have seen such aids self-destructing in the trunk of a salesperson's car, but I did not need to see that to know who was or who was not using the sales aids we furnished. The orders written told that story.

One company for which I worked was especially good at supplying sales aids. I remember an interest-getter that was as effective as it was simple. Right after World War II, rayon cord replaced the cotton tension member in automotive fan belts. My employer had a small card (about 3 inches by 4 inches) prepared telling briefly the story about rayon and its many advantages for this new application. There was a short piece of the rayon cord, exactly like that used in the belts, attached to the card.

The man who took me around the territory on my introduction carried a pocket full of these cards and every time we met someone, he handed that person one, sometimes before we had even exchanged pleasantries. The reactions amazed me. The recipients almost fondled the card with its rayon cord; they tried to break or stretch the cord and then they read the message while still twisting the cord through their fingers. During all of that time, they asked a jillion questions, and every one of them evidenced real interest and spontaneous respect for the new development. I could not believe, and am still amazed, how that simple thing could open the way for serious sales discussion.

During my stint with this same company, it was later my misfortune that they gave me a sample to carry that weighed about forty pounds (that is early in the day, much more by day's end). Through an unusual requirement, I wound up one time carrying this thing from Abilene to Odessa, Texas on the train. When I sat down with my fellow seat occupant, he asked, "What in the world is that?" When I told him, he replied, "I almost wish I could use one of those."

Even now I have the sensation that my right arm is still a little longer than my left from lugging that thing all over west Texas. And I know that it ruined my golf game because I frequently get so much right arm into my swing that I hook many shots plumb out of the course.

Again, use whatever sales aids you have until they prove ineffective. And if your company is derelict in furnishing them, rustle up your own. There are plenty in every district warehouse or general office—small products or parts, old photos, brochures, or something that you can show a prospect that will catch his or her interest better than anything you can say.

If you have nothing to offer but conversation, have a provocative question ready for each prospect. Make it one that will force the prospect to think about your subject and compel him or her to give you some helpful information in the answer.

2. Introduce Your Company

Early on you have to introduce your company if your prospect does not already know about it. Enlarge on what you might have told him or her in the first step. Tell the prospect about important points of your company's history with emphasis on accomplishments and present status in your field. A short film developed by some companies is especially effective for this.

If it is an old customer, bring him or her up to date on every new development that will benefit that customer and remind him or her occasionally about your past accomplishments that are still relevant. Embellish all you say with any aids you have or any unique and relevant examples of recent sales and applications.

Try to accomplish this much, at least:

1. Tell the basic story of what your company is and what it can do, and
2. Give the customer evidence that your record has been established. In short, make the customer fully aware of what you can do for him or her and how well you can do it.

3. Sell Yourself

It is too early to fully accomplish this for a new prospect but it is none too soon to be aware of the need. The impression you create was started the minute you met the prospect, but his or her evaluation of you is a gradual, continuing, and subtle process. The best advice for you is to be yourself and do your own thing.

You need not win a popularity contest among all suppliers, but you do need to gain the respect of your customers and prospects. A passing grade is required on these points:

Knowledge of your product.
Ability to help your prospective buyer.
Proof of your dependability.
Evidence of your integrity.

4. Determine Prospect's General Needs

As soon as possible learn all you can about the requirements of your prospect, at least in a general way.

5. Sell Your Product Line

Cite the advantages of your products, emphasizing those in which any interest has been expressed.

6. Determine or Create Specific Need

These three (4, 5, and 6) are distinctive enough in some respects to deserve individual labels, but they are closely related and will probably be developed together in most cases.

Your primary objective now is to learn all you can about your customer, particularly his or her needs, and the more specifically the better.

Introduce as much of your product line as you can in each session, expanding whatever evokes interest.

Give your prospect time to react. In fact, plan your discussion to draw him or her out as much as possible. Ask a lot of questions and watch this individual's reactions. Pursue any interest displayed to determine exactly what attracts him or her. Then talk about your products that relate to that interest.

Meet as many people as you can. Learn about their purchasing process, if possible. Get a plant tour if you are able to.

If you cannot find a specific need, try to create one.

7. Satisfy That Need

If you are fortunate enough in this effort to learn about a specific purchase that is pending, try for the order. Failing that, begin your campaign to sell it. Suggest and describe applications of your equipment and present the important options.

After you leave, plan your strategy for a major sales campaign to get that pending order.

8. Complete the Selling Job

In your next calls, confirm your equipment selection and begin to reduce options to avoid confusion.

Meet all who will be involved in the purchase and begin to evaluate their clout. Tell them the full story. Answer their questions and hammer hard on the advantages of what you offer.

9. Overcome Objections; Close Sale

Now is the time to clear all remaining questions, dispel any lingering doubts, strengthen weak points, emphasize the strong ones, and satisfy all objections. (See Chapter Five, Objections.)

If no opportunity to close has yet come up, move into your closing effort. (See Chapter Six, Closing the Sale.)

GENERAL CONSIDERATIONS

While there are many common elements in all presentations, no two ever develop in exactly the same manner. Flexibility in meeting special situations is necessary, but that is what adds the professional dimension to selling, and therein lies its challenge and its opportunity.

Bear in mind that many sales cannot be closed in just one call but, regardless of your discussion with buying personnel, ask for some kind of order every time.

For the new prospect, most of the steps of the presentation are required. Provide as much of an overview of your company, its products, and its capabilities as possible during that first visit. Iterate and expand that on the ensuing calls.

Consider, too, that there is a unique risk of sudden termination at each point. If you fail to create interest early, your effort will be unproductive, and this is true even though your listener might be too polite to cut you short. There is also that same hazard in each step that follows when you are trying to attract a new prospect.

For the regular call on a steady customer, it is obvious that less repetition is required. In fact, too much could become boring. On the other hand, avoid becoming blasé about your steady, reliable customers. Presentations to them should not be shoddily planned or unenthusiastically executed. You must be ever attentive to what they are doing and planning. Think how embarrassed you would be to learn about a proposed project from an outsider.

Be careful, too, about too much visiting with the customers who are also good friends. Your competitor who shares no common interest with them will be discussing his or her products and scoring points with them.

Except for the first call, most others can have some element of followup, or they should have. That subject is treated separately in Chapter Seven.

Calls can vary in another important respect. They can be one-on-one with a lone buyer or they can be meetings with a large group. Whenever possible, you need to know what to expect so that you can make appropriate plans.

There is one presentation that is especially important and that merits the full attention given to it under the next major heading—THE MAJOR PRESENTATION.

That is the one for the final meeting with a large group that is making its final decision about a large purchase, whether it be equipment for a major plant expansion, a long-term supply contract, a new distributor franchise, or some other large-volume requirement.

For such a really good prospect, no professional salesperson would gather up whatever happened to be handy as he or she rushed out of the office in nervous haste to conduct a presentation.

The detailed discussion is developed to help those who hope to and expect to encounter such prospects. It will also serve to exemplify some of the points already considered and to tie them together in a working session on paper. In a sense, it will add the HOW to the WHAT and the WHY.

With slight modification, this same presentation can be used as a model for other requirements, not necessarily all sales. For example, there are also many good suggestions for planning and conducting Sales and Training Meetings.

Remember This

In sales you must expect to encounter a great variety of requirements. Be flexible enough to adapt to each.

In each case consider your purpose, your audience, and the subject to be presented. Contemplate what your listeners need to hear and conduct your planning and presentation to suit the need.

THE MAJOR PRESENTATION

There are two phases of preparation to include both the preparation in advance of the meeting and the final details on the meeting day at the meeting site.

Advance Preparation

1. Complete details of the meeting site, date, time, and those who will attend. Schedule an important meeting in a hotel if you can, to ensure adequate facilities and to minimize interruptions.

Make all reservations as soon as details are approved and before you leave the prospect's city.

If you cannot determine exactly who will attend, assume that it will be all whom you have met in your sales calls thus far.

2. Set your specific goals for the meeting in detail.

Naturally you want to make the sale. That is your goal, but during your preparation, you have to break it down into smaller, more specific elements.

Considering your audience, spell out as clearly as possible what you must accomplish to make the sale. For example, there are certain facts that must be firmly established, complex aspects of your proposal must be clarified, objections must be overcome, and some individuals may need further convincing.

3. Decide what help you will need and enlist that now so that you may detail the responsibilities of those individuals and use their help in your planning.

The purpose of the help should be your best guide as to whom you will need. If your product is highly specialized or technical, include a specialist. If a lease or other financial instrument is involved, try to get the person who knows all of the ramifications, someone who has authority to negotiate on the spot.

You can always use some good sales help. While one person is talking, the other can observe the reactions and better judge the progress, deciding which points are accepted and which need more emphasis.

To summarize, you need everyone there whose absence could jeopardize your chances to close the deal at this meeting.

4. Prepare an agenda. For a really important session before a large group, it can be very beneficial to have a formal agenda to include in a binder to be given to those who attend. The very least it will do is to show that you have prepared thoroughly. It flatters your audience by showing them that they deserve your best effort.

Even more beneficial is the opportunity to enumerate all of the points to be covered and the sequence that will be most helpful to you.

Show a break or two at strategic points. Time them to disrupt you least. Avoid any interruption during your final closing push.

5. Gather your support material—samples, models, application photos, brochures, catalogs and price lists, technical bulletins, performance records, studies of production costs of your equipment, unique application stories, awards to your company, customer endorsements, and anything else your imagination suggests might be helpful.

Undoubtedly your company has lots of such things and other sales tools as well, such as slides, films, film strips, and flip charts. Consider all that you have and take all you might need even if you do not use them all.

One especially desirable sales aid is a short film or slide series on the history and record of your company. Even if you have covered the story in parts before, it makes a nice summation to establish a mood for the meeting.

Be sure to include the necessary projectors and other equipment, along with spare parts and extension cords. Take tape, tacks, and any hand tools you need to set up models or displays.

6. Write out your speech. This part of your preparation is to guarantee that you will include all that you must cover in the most effective order and that you will carefully select your words and phrases. It is also needed to show those who will work with you what you will say and when.

Aim for clarity and conciseness. You are trying to reduce generalities to specifics and to present a brief, lucid summary of what you have covered in your other calls. Keep your language plain and simple.

Work into your presentation the sales tools and other supports you will display or use. Include stimulants to audience participation. It is best to use all devices such as these early in your presentation to avoid disruption during your closing segment.

Inject a little humor when you can—not bawdy stories but something to lend variety and change of pace to what is probably a dull subject in spite of its vital interest to all.

For the large meeting, assume that you will stand at a podium and address a sizable group unless you know otherwise. Or you might be at the head of a large conference table. Think of the formality of such a session and prepare mentally for it. One time a salesman and I had an appointment with a prospect where we expected to meet one or two in an informal discussion. When we got there, we were ushered into a large, impressive conference room where eighteen of them were already present. I can tell you that the initial shock of such a surprise reception can throw one momentarily off stride.

7. Practice your presentation. Even memorize parts of it if that makes you feel comfortable. Have your opening and closing sections well in mind. If you do commit parts to memory, deliver those parts as casually as you can, not as you would a declamation before a speech class.

For many a meeting, I actually recited aloud to myself what I planned to say as I drove the seemingly endless miles between calls. That was when I was traveling a territory in the expansive Southwest, where between Carlsbad and El Paso, for example, and plenty of other stretches as well, there was never a bigger distraction than a jackrabbit bounding across the highway.

I had another lesson in how important it is to practice a presentation. With two companies that involved the delivery of our divisional business plan each year to the top people in the executive office. Those are elaborate productions and well they should be, considering that they make up the company's blueprint for ensuring a successful year. It was my good fortune that both of these companies considered a presentation to a prospect just as important, and we prepared for them in the same manner.

8. Assemble anything you plan to incorporate in the binder or to just pass out. Many companies have a binder or portfolio for just this purpose. It adds a certain flair and a suggestion of professionalism as well as providing a cover for the data to be distributed.

For those who want to make up such a binder, there is more in Appendix A, page 175.

9. When all of your program has been planned, meet with your helpers and go over that plan.

Also consider all of the objections that may come up. Prepare to meet those objections and make sure that you have all you will need to overcome them. Chapter Five is devoted to objections.

10. Prepare a contract or something a prospect can sign.

11. At this time, it would be wise to make a checklist of all of the things you still have to do before the meeting. Include with it a list of everything you must take from the office.

12. Reconfirm all reservations. If you are planning to rent a projector, make sure that it will be reserved for you, too.

On-Site Preparation

On the day of your meeting for a major sales presentation for a big order before a prestigious group, jump out of bed with a special air of expectancy. You have a very big job this day and also a very big opportunity.

Be at the meeting site in plenty of time to ensure that you can check and complete all final arrangements. Make it at least two hours before the scheduled start.

Study the actual physical arrangement of the room. Decide about a seating plan. (Classroom style is very good for a large group.) Visualize how you will use the equipment, and position it to facilitate your delivery. Complete an arrangement that will make you comfortable doing what you have to do.

That sense of well-being has always been important to me. During one of the business plan meetings to which I referred earlier in this chapter, the audience was a very august group of new employers. I knew that I could not feel at ease the way it was all arranged. The podium was on the wrong end of the big conference table, but there had been no chance to ask that it be changed before we went on.

When my turn came, I went to the podium, picked it up, and moved it to the other end. Eyebrows shot upward and quizzical glances were exchanged, but before anyone could ask what in the world I was doing, I said, "I think I can do a better job for you from this end." I felt easy and everyone else eased back in their chairs. After the meeting, one of the most austere of those attending congratulated me. He was the one whose eyebrows had elevated the most.

Such seemingly insignificant details have always been important to me. I need to feel comfortable for speaking seriously before a large group.

I used to think that I might be some kind of nut on the subject until I read a textbook that treated persuasive discourse under the general topic of rhetoric.

There was a section devoted to the use of space as it related to formal and informal discussion. The point was that relative positions of one to the other of the participants and the distance between them had a great influence on the tone of the interchange among the participants. That comforted me to know that it might be important. It also suggested that if rhetoricians are canny enough to observe such factors, maybe salespersons could learn from them.

Place the binders around the table. Consider that placement that will work most in your favor. Usually people will sit in the spot designated.

You cannot always tell who the heckler(s) will be, but if you suspect one, seat him or her between a couple of those who will in your judgment be good supporters. They can have only a good influence on the heckler and might quiet him or her. In fact, position strategically throughout the seating arrangement those who you think favor your proposal. Place some at the far end of a long table to break up any possibly distracting group.

Set up any displays and hang posters or other things you have to dress up the room and attract attention to your product. Assemble all models or other working tools. Create a festive atmosphere. Try to ensure that the minute the listeners come into the room, they will sense that it will not be the same boring session they last attended.

I am indebted to a good friend for that idea. He was, and as far as I know still is, the training director and a general utility person for important functions for a large corporation. He never held a meeting of any importance for a sales prospect without trying to endow the room with a sense of purpose.

We held a meeting one time for a prospective distributor. We arrived at the motel a couple of hours early. We plastered every wall of the meeting room with application photos, posters, ad reprints, and other gimmicks, and we covered two large tables with samples of our products, catalogs, and training aids. To him, a major presentation should be turned into a production. I was not that impressed until I heard the comments and we signed the distributor.

Place your equipment and check it. Assume that everything that can go wrong will, as Murphy swore it would. Run the projectors and make sure that they are focused and sychronized for instant startup. Check again that you have spare parts such as lamps for the projectors.

Get your notes in order and then go to the podium and run through your opening. Get a feel for what to expect. It can boost your confidence.

As your last preparation gesture before the meeting starts, go to the restroom, give yourself a critical inspection before the mirror, then pull yourself up to your full height and tell yourself that you are ready. Then, go sell that big order.

Remember This

Before any important sales presentation, sit down and think about it. Run through it in detail just as you plan to conduct it.

Take notes as you go concerning the preparation each step will require.

Then review, expand, and summarize the notes for your guide to the preparation needed.

The better you prepare, the better your sales effort, and the greater your chance for success.

Execution

A sales presentation is really nothing more than a nonstop closing effort. The very fact that you have been given time by a prospect indicates his or her consideration of a purchase. That should be your inspiration to do your best.

OPENING.   The first item on your agenda should be the introduction of all of those who are present. Arrange beforehand for the prospect's key person to introduce his or her people and explain the purpose of the meeting.

Thank him or her for this introduction and then for the privilege of being there. Thank all of those there for the time they are giving you.

Introduce your personnel and explain what they will cover during the presentation. Invite all to ask questions at any time from any of your people if that is your desire.

This is a good time to thumb through the binders or anything that you have passed out. They probably have already picked them up, and unless you describe them briefly now, they will probably still be looking them over when you are ready to start.

AROUSING INTEREST.   Your next concern is to arouse interest. This is the real start of your meeting and you need a strong start.

Some are effective telling a story. For others this is a very bad technique. Recall from your own experience on the other side your reaction to a speaker who started by doing a very poor job of telling a story you had already heard from a skilled raconteur. Unless you, too, are a skilled story teller, use some other opening.

Use the one you have prepared and deliver it as forcefully as you can.

This is an excellent time to show a good film about the history of your company and its progress to your position of today. If you do not have that, get immediately into your own story of the company and its contributions to industry.

ENTHUSIASM.   Show lots of enthusiasm, especially at the start. Appear excited about the meeting. Both enthusiasm and excitement are contagious.

Without displaying any conceit or giving any impression of superiority, show all of the confidence you can. Make it impossible for your audience to fail to see that you know your product, that you are a professional salesperson, and that you are there to sell something.

MANNER OF SPEAKING.   Be crisp and forceful in your speaking. Above all, avoid a drab monotone that can only indicate that you are half bored with the job at hand. Be especially careful to be stimulating in those portions that you have memorized.

Speak as clearly as you can and be alert for any signal suggesting confusion by any of the listeners. If you notice someone who looks lost, ask if he or she has a question, but avoid asking in a way that might embarrass or humiliate that individual.

It is unwise to curse when you are making a sales presentation of any kind. You might offend the listener. For some reason profanity is not as acceptable or tolerable from a podium as it might be later over a beer. It is unfortunate that curse words are so objectionable since they are so universally expressive and so uniquely emphatic. There are some situations where they seem almost indispensable.

Think of your speech as a program of entertainment. It really is a performance, and if you have any flair for the theatrical, put it to use. It will enliven your delivery.

DESCRIPTION.   Regardless of the visual aids and props you have, some parts of your speaking will entail plain description and that can be the dullest of all. Use a model, sample, picture, or diagram whenever you can and work with a blackboard or a flip chart to simplify as much as possible. It is not a time to confuse with a lot of technical jargon or ambiguous doublespeak.

Talk to the level of your audience. You will not insult the most educated in the group by using monosyllables, but you will lose some if you are not clear and concise.

SUSTAINING INTEREST.   Constantly gauge the reaction of your listeners. A nod here or a puzzled expression there will tell you a lot. Key in on those who you find are the most expressive in their reactions to tell you how you are being received. Make any corrections indicated.

Do what you have to do to sustain interest and remember that it will flag most during the middle part of your discourse. You might need to inject a question or two, or pass and discuss a handout. If your audience looks too bored, call for a brief stretch in place or take a break. There should be a scheduled break no less frequently than every two hours.

DISPLAY.   A display is a good device for stimulating interest. It is also an effective aid in explaining a complicated feature. Use the real thing unless it is too big, too special, or just not available. If you must settle for less, make sure that the replica loses none of the character of the original. For example, if you are demonstrating the flexibility of a new hose product with just a short length, be careful to make it long enough to be as flexible as the full length.

EXAMPLES.   Everyone is interested in what others are doing, especially if those others have been successful where they themselves have failed. Tell your audience about your customers who have solved difficult problems with your equipment. Cite those who have the best reputations and the most prestige in the industry. Give plenty of detail, but be discreet about any of the others' operations that might be considered confidential. Your prospect might fear that you will later divulge some of his or her secrets.

PARTICIPATION. A very productive technique for enlivening a presentation is to involve the audience. Participation makes the listeners more attentive to the points you are trying to make and they feel that they are sharing in your effort.

It also facilitates your ongoing analysis of how you are doing and what subjects need to be better covered. It will afford you the best clue about where to place your closing emphasis. It might also indicate when you can make an attempt to close the sale, and you need to do that at the very first opportunity, even if you have not completed your much-studied plan.

Ask for comments as you conclude a portion of your discussion. If general requests do not produce results, ask someone directly, naturally someone who apparently agrees with what you have been saying.

HECKLERS. It is almost inevitable that any audience of more than six or eight will have at least one heckler, more for bigger groups. I think of a heckler as a person who is going to antagonize as much as possible, regardless of the justification; that individual gets his or her kicks that way.

At least three motives might inspire the heckler. He or she does not like the speaker, and this dislike can be spontaneous and unjustified; the heckler is insecure and must monopolize the scene to gain attention; or at times, the heckler is not a human but a part of a horse—the part which inexplicably is more numerous than the natural ratio of one per animal.

I think it is better to have two hecklers than just one. When there are two, there is a good chance that one will see how ridiculous he or she appears when the other is doing the heckling and might give up quickly. Then the other, having lost support, might do the same.

When you have a heckler to deal with, keep your cool. And avoid argument or belligerence. The clearest success for a heckler is to visibly upset the speaker. If at all possible, the heckler should just be ignored.

Sometimes a heckler will ask a question designed to embarrass the speaker rather than to seek information. If you can do so gracefully, respond something like this, "That's a good question. I plan to cover that subject a little later." Then forget about it. It probably will not be brought up again.

There are more extreme techniques. Sometimes the heckler will not stop until he or she gets your agreement on some point or another. Agree with reservations and then at some later point, after the heckler has settled down, correct any false impressions your original accord might have created.

A humorous comment will break the tension a heckler can cause. But it can be harmful if it is insulting or critical. Even the heckler is one of them, and some of them will come to the rescue if he or she gets into too much trouble.

There might be a time when you will just have to ignore the heckler. The most inoffensive way to do that is to fake unawareness of what is said.

The best lessons on how to handle hecklers can be learned from politicians. They are frequently facing hostile audiences that usually have some members who will resort to any technique to embarrass or discredit them.

One of the very best at coping with hecklers is President Reagan. During the 1980 presidential campaign, his defenses became clear. First, he always smiled when some unsympathetic remark or question was expressed. He also would, with no apparent loss of support, ignore the question or answer it with a long and totally irrelevant reply. But his most memorable technique in one extreme case was to reply with a very direct suggestion to the heckler, "Aw, shut up!" That was direct handling. It was also ingenious. It drew a lot of sympathy and support, probably because when he said it, he did so without any rancor whatsoever.

One thing you can always look forward to is that sooner or later a heckler will shut up—maybe sooner if you have been able to seat him or her between two of your good supporters.

TEAMWORK. Having more than one in a presentation provides an excellent opportunity for an interesting change of pace. The speaking can be shared, with each taking the part for which he or she has the best training and most experience.

As already mentioned, the continuing analysis that is possible with two or more speakers, which can help so much in the closing effort, is an even more important benefit of teamwork.

OBJECTIONS. Chapter Five is devoted entirely to objections—meeting them as they come up, anticipating them, and overcoming them. Little need be said here except to emphasize the aspects especially applicable to the meeting.

It is hoped that you have foreseen most of the objections and have planned your strategy before this final meeting. That was one of your goals during all of your previous sales efforts. At this stage, objections should not be totally defeating. The prospect has been evaluating your proposal thoroughly, and it is unlikely that you would be here if there were many critical stumbling blocks.

You might expect in a group like this that some eager beaver who has not had much chance to say anything will raise a prickly question just to get some credit from his or her boss for participating. The best answer for that question is something like this, "Yes, that's a fair question. I think Jack was referring to something like that before and I think we settled it then, didn't we Jack?" Jack will appreciate the attention and will probably agree with you. If it will help, you might recap if the points were similar at all. If not, handle the question as an individual item.

Another technique might work in a group if an objection stumps you momentarily. Just reply, "I really don't know about that. It has never come up before." Then follow with questions to the others: What do the rest of you think about that? Is that a problem? How much problem could it be? What could be done to eliminate it? Most frequently, the objection will be overruled. If it is not, then you have gained a better knowledge of the problem and an insight to some of the answers.

If a serious objection is raised at this stage and you cannot answer it, ask for a recess. Huddle with your team and see if you can work it out.

If you cannot do that, call your office for help. Check with the engineers. If you have a service organization, solicit ideas from them. Ask for references of others who might have met and solved the problem. If all else fails, find out what concessions can be offered. The possibilities might be a special warranty provision if the expected trouble develops, a credit allowance for repair parts, or even a price concession immediately against the contingency.

After all of the possible alternatives have been authorized, arrange a negotiating session with the top people only. This will carry an implication that the meeting has been finished and that the order is now contingent only upon the resolution of this last objection.

Keep the group as small as possible to facilitate agreement. If no clear solution is found, ask for the order anyway and concede that the buyer may put a reasonable condition on its face relative to the one controversial point. You must make every reasonable effort to get some written commitment at this time. Otherwise, all other bidders might be called back.

That sounds like a tenuous agreement but it does give you the opportunity to take it back to study with all of your officials. In effect, you have gained refusal of the order.

The Close

The close is a subject unto itself and is presented in Chapter Six.

Toward the end of your presentation, you should have a good idea where you stand and you should be able to detect closing invitations. When you do, make your move and close the sale.

If it is still not quite that simple, you might feel that a brief summary is in order, much like the final appeal to the jury by a trial lawyer. Keep your summary brief and repeat the points that have been best received. Iterate some of the comments any of the audience made that indicated their approval. In the final analysis, closing is merely eliminating doubt about the rectitude of the decision to buy, provided that was the intention of the prospect in the first place.

When you have finished your summation, bring out your contract or proposal and review any subordinate details relating to schedule, mode of shipment, terms, and so on. Then present your copy of the proposal to the prospect for signature.

Congratulations! You sold a big order.

BE A PRO

Whatever your presentation requirements, analyze the special needs and adapt to them.

In all respects—planning, preparing, executing—do your very best. If your maximum effort is not justified, make some other call.

Successful salespersons are really just winners. They try to win every time, and to do that, they use every means they can imagine. They do not count on receiving breaks; they make their own.

chapter five

Objections

Because they are so misunderstood and yet so inevitable,
objections merit special attention.

THE NATURE OF OBJECTIONS

In the sales sense, an objection is any response or criticism by a prospect that threatens to jeopardize, or render impossible, the consummation of a sale.

Major and Minor Objections

A major objection is one that has a reasonably strong and logical basis, at least in the mind of the objector. It is normally genuine and sincere. In most cases, no order will be placed until it has been resolved or subordinated. Major objections must be met head-on by the salesperson.

    A minor objection is not as well grounded or as relevant and sometimes is merely a ruse or cover-up for some reason to delay commitment of an order. Sometimes it will evaporate in the face of an aggressive and effective sales presentation or an exceptionally strong response on a major objection.

The Fear Element

As much as anything, objections are usually expressions of fear. The buyer fears that the product will not work satisfactorily and remembers the headaches he or she had when something recently purchased failed to live up to expectations.

Sometimes the buyer is afraid that the supplier will not be willing or able to help when trouble does arise and can recall when that has happened. At other times, the buyer just lacks confidence in all salespersons, believing that most of them are prone to exaggerate.

Then, the buyer always has doubt that the best price has been quoted. That doubt is ingrained into the nature of a buyer, as any salesperson knows who has ever seen the sign that hangs in many purchasing offices, saying PURCHASING IS A PROFIT-MAKING DIVISION.

Reactions to Objections

To many salespersons, especially the inexperienced, objections indicate a totally unfavorable and ominous reaction foreboding inevitable failure for them. They often bristle as if the objection were a harsh personal insult or a very unkind and unfair criticism of their product and their company. They suffer an instant loss of composure and with it their capability to cope with what is little more than a common reaction by a serious buyer.

Two questions might help salespersons to fend off such a reaction. All they must do is ask themselves: Would anyone who has absolutely no interest in them, or their product, or their company raise an objection about any of them? Would the salespersons rather have one of their best sales presentations be greeted with an objection or with complete silence?

They should also consider the reaction of the real sales pro who sees an objection as a sign of progress and welcomes it as an invitation to move to close an order.

Whatever objections are, they do present minor problems. They delay somewhat the final signing of an order. And the least they can mean is that some salesperson is going to have to start thinking and go to work. In spite of what he or she had hoped and expected, the salesperson is going to have to earn this order.

Remember This

The significant thing about objection is that they indicate interest on the part of the prospect and often a readiness to place an order.

That interest means that it is time for the salesperson to dispel the doubt and proceed with an aggressive effort to close the sale.

RESPONSE TO OBJECTIONS—GENERAL

Attitude

In my judgment, the first step of the response to an objection is the assumption of the proper attitude. Be composed. If you are slightly miffed at what seems an unfair criticism, think of it as a favor to you that the objection has been openly expressed.

Assume an air of confidence that indicates that you see no problem in satisfying any doubts of the prospect. Did you ever hear about a good doctor who showed any less composure upon discovery that a patient had a really serious problem? Take a lesson in professionalism from the most skillful of all.

Even if you are caught completely off guard by an objection you have never heard before, try not to show it. If you cannot immediately see how to proceed, ask questions with the hope that the answers will afford a clue or more clearly define the problem.

If necessary, stall for time by changing the subject so the objector will have to do most of the talking while you concentrate on your plan to dispel the objection.

Analysis

Analyze the objection to determine precisely what it is, how serious it is, and what refutation might be plausible. To help you do this, there are several questions you can ask yourself or your listener. Here are some examples:

Ask yourself—Is the objection real?

Is it sound and logical?

Have you heard it before?

Is it the real objection?

What could be its basis?

Ask the objector—What does he or she really mean?

What problem does he or she foresee?

Why?

Has there been a problem like it before?

How does *he or she* think it may be solved?

Give your prospect plenty of time to answer your questions. Wait for a full reply that might reveal a clue for your answer.

In making an analysis, one should consider that the real objection is not always the one that is offered. If you suspect that, gradually modify your response to cover what you think the real problem is.

There is a natural reluctance for some critics to be too harsh when the complaint is serious or seems to be most offensive. Make the critic state the worst. The mere expression of it might mitigate it to him or her. After hearing the worst, the critic may well think that it is not as bad as it sounds. Then, too, when you have satisfied the worst, you have satisfied it all.

Reaction

Avoid overreaction to objections. Employ a logical, credible refutation as simply as you can, not an overpowering barrage of words. You have everything to lose and nothing to gain by rushing into your reply by nervously saying what comes to mind first. If what you say is unreasonable, the prospect will see that and all confidence in you will be destroyed. If he or she accepts what you say and it later proves incorrect, you stand to lose a customer.

Take it easy, but avoid treating an objection lightly. A good opening for your response could be something like, "Mr. Jones, that's a reasonable concern but . . . . "

Consider, too, that since fear might be a large part of the objection, you should be patient, tolerant, and sympathetic. Fortunately for all salespersons, fear is based on a lack of knowledge or a misunderstanding. The prescription for either should be clear to a thinking salesperson—correct and clarify inaccurate or inadequate knowledge or impressions.

Above all, avoid argument. The prospect will eventually concede an argument, and you will easily win by default. But you will also lose the important thing, the order.

It is inevitable that sooner or later you will encounter an objection for which you have no ready answer. If that happens at a time when you sense that the prospect is anxious to buy, you might be tempted to fake an answer. That would be a serious mistake.

If you have no idea what to say, say so. It is no sin to admit that you do not know. At least, that will sound like an honest answer.

But even then you do not have to give up. Go on to say that you will find out. If the need is urgent, call the office, and after you have found someone who can help you and you have explained the situation, get your prospect on the line with you. If your helper back at the office satisfies the objection, you will not even have to ask for the order. Just ask the buyer, "How do you want that shipped? What is your order number?"

If time is not a critical factor, ask the buyer to delay the purchase until you can return with an answer, and tell him or her when that will be. When you have the solution and all of the other ammunition you need, *take* it back to the buyer and complete the sale.

Remember This

In the face of objections, keep cool.

Give full consideration and sympathy to the objection, but avoid overreaction.

Dispel the prospect's fears and move quickly to close the sale.

RESPONSE TO OBJECTIONS—SPECIFIC

Of all of the objections to placing an order by a prospect, seven are most common. If others arise, the suggestions for solving these seven will probably facilitate your handling of the unexpected ones. The seven are

1. Price   5. Buyer Indecision
2. Product   6. Buyer Inertia
3. Service   7. Buyer Delay
4. Company

Price

Price is the most discussed element of a purchase. It is given more attention than it merits, and much of that is the fault of the salesperson. How
many in sales have opened an interview with, "Boy, have I got a deal for
you, today!" or, "I've got a new price on _____ that you can't turn
down."

It is inexcusable for a salesperson to exaggerate the importance of
price. It should be realized that if the basis for all buying were reduced to
price, there would be no need for salespersons. All a supplier would have
to do is mail out the briefest of catalogs and price lists with special
mailings for those "deals" and "new prices." And the additional jobs in
the postal system to handle all of those mailings would fall far short of
enough for all of those displaced salespersons.

Very rarely should price even be mentioned first. When a salesperson
starts with price, it is an admission that there is little else to offer. It is also
an insult to the prospect in the sense that it suggests that price is his or her
only concern, too.

Price should be the last subject to come up, because unless all other
conditions have been satisfied and all objections eliminated, the price is
academic. Even if the buyer asks the price early in the discussion, it is wise
to delay the answer with a simple, polite, "If you don't mind, let me get to
that later," or some equally inoffensive stall. The sound of the price to a
buyer will be one thing before you have established the superiority of your
product and something quite different after you have done that. And
when price is involved, that first impression can be difficult to change.

If you are especially sensitive about price, think of the many sales
that are made, even in this cost-conscious age, in which the price is merely
a casual consideration mentioned toward the end of the negotiations only
for completion of the paper work.

When there is an indication of a price problem, it must be determined whether it is based on a prospect's hunch or general feeling or
whether the prospect does actually have a lower offer on a specific need.
Ask questions to settle that first.

If the prospect's reply indicates that he or she merely thinks you are high, there are several things you can do. Express the real cost in terms other than the initial cost, and cite an example if you can. If manufacturing equipment is involved, show the prospect how your machinery has saved others money. Tell him what they have said about the savings they have realized. Arrange a telephone contact to one of your boosters.

Discuss your product in more detail with emphasis on its Cadillac features. Show the prospect product qualities that are more costly to produce and explain the advantages they offer. Compare some of the features of competitive products that exemplify less attention to quality than economy of production. But make any points involving competitors without being too critical.

I was with a district manager in Chicago one time calling on a prospect who really seemed bothered about price but who would not give us any specific details. The district manager finally asked him, "Would you please give us an example where we're high? Maybe we can show you that our product is still a better buy."

The prospect slowly, begrudgingly answered that he had seen our latest financial statement and that any company in our business that made all of that money had to be high priced.

My coworker jumped on that immediately. "Mr. Jones, I have a copy of that report, and I would like to call your attention to some other figures in it. Did you notice our assets, especially that cash we have on hand? Did you see that small figure for liabilities? We'll be here to help you tomorrow and the day after that if you ever have any problem with anything you buy from us."

I got into the act. "Look at our sales figures on page 7, Mr. Jones. They have increased every year. But the most important thing about them is not shown. According to the figures we get from the association for our industry, our sales are increasing faster than those of any competitor. We're getting a larger market share, and we could not do that by overcharging our customers. Our company sees nothing sinful in making money, and we know that we can do a better job for you when we do."

His delayed reaction was a thoughtful statement, "Maybe you're right." We did not sell anything that day, but he became a good customer later.

If a competitor has offered a significantly lower price, find out what it is and what the competitor offers for that price. To the new person in sales, that sounds like a formidable job. But if he or she has been convincing in his or her sales efforts, the information will be easy to get. The more desirable the product has been made, the more information will be given and the easier to overcome the price objection.

Carefully compare the products or services bid. Are they the same "or equal," as claimed? The chances are that they are not exactly the same, and even the slightest difference can make them unequal, even the cash discount.

One time one of our salespersons sold a conveying system to a large meat packer just starting in the Midwest, after it seemed that we were out of the running because our price was higher than a competitive bid. When he called to tell me that he had the order, he was ecstatic.

I asked him how he had overcome the price disadvantage. He told me that right down the line it looked as if we were both quoting identical equipment. Then the prospect mentioned that there was actually an added savings on freight because their equipment was lighter. That immediately suggested to our representative that if ours weighed more, then it had to be better somewhere.

They reviewed the bid again, even more carefully, and finally discovered that one of the important components in our offer was indeed fabricated from heavier gauge steel. Since this component was subject to great wear, and since it comprised a significant part of the total machinery, our bid was considered better and the order was committed on the spot.

In comparing prices against a specific competitor, be fair and objective, not critical. If an item-by-item check cannot be made, there is nothing unfair about comments like these, "Mr. Jones, ABC Company seems to be stressing their low price. Are you sure that their equipment will do what ours will. You know that the savings will be worthless if it doesn't." Then you might even add, "We haven't found them to be very much of a factor in most areas." That is really catty, but if it is true, it passes my test.

In both the daily newspapers and on the TV newscasts between December 12 and 15, 1981, a very curious development among Christmas shoppers was given considerable mention and should give heart to salespersons faced with a price objection. In spite of the increasing unemployment and an economic outlook that was becoming bleaker by the day, shoppers were buying higher-quality, higher-priced gifts even though they supposedly had less money to spend.

Sometimes it is necessary to reduce a price to meet a low bid. In fact, it is done every day in some industries for some types of sales. When it is necessary, try to give a reason for the concession for an immediate commitment to justify shading your price without destroying the integrity of your pricing policy or setting a bothersome precedent.

Some possibilities are:

Your chance to buy materials to gain better prices and to hedge against inflation.

The possibility of fitting the project more advantageously into your production schedule.

The opportunity to fill a slack schedule in one or more departments.

Any of those could be good reasons for a concession in price and would avoid causing your prospect to wonder why you had not offered it earlier.

Product

Overcoming objections about your product should be fairly simple if your company is quality-minded and if the application you have recommended is sound. Try to find out the actual features that your prospect considers unsatisfactory and the exact basis for those feelings. The latter may include rumor, impression, or actual experience, and two of those are pretty weak.

Tell the prospect more about your production facilities and methods. Explain how you do things to avoid causing the very difficulty he or she fears. For example, if concentricity for any element of a part is critical, tell the prospect about the jigs and fixtures you use to guarantee that concentricity. Use parts and samples if applicable to demonstrate.

Tell the prospect what others have said about your quality and their success with your equipment. Challenge the prospect to verify your statements and help him or her do that. Call a satisfied customer and let the prospect talk to him or her.

If the objection is deep-seated, offer a special guarantee on a trial order. Let the prospect spell out the special provisions on the order. Take the order contingent upon acceptance of your company.

If the order is large and the doubt lingers, invite the prospect to visit your plant at your expense to meet your key people and to see just how you manufacture your products. If he or she cannot come, take your technical people to the prospect's office to lend you their expertise and authority.

We had a prospect in Colorado Springs who purchased from a competitor on a yearly contract large quantities of components like we made. One year we were finally able to get on the bid list. Through close follow-up, our salesman learned that our price was competitive and that the present supplier was not entirely acceptable. Yet we did not get the order. As it turned out, the reason was that the buyer and other purchasing department personnel did not know enough about our company.

During the year, we were able to furnish a few special items that were not covered by the contract. When we received an invitation to bid on the following year's needs, we were able to persuade the purchasing agent and the production manager to visit our plant. While they were there, we finalized the contract. For the rest of the years I knew about, we were able to renew the contract each year through negotiation, and they did not send out bid invitations.

Remember This

Tackle price problems by thoroughly selling your prospect on your product first.

Then determine the specific price disadvantage and prove that your product is worth the difference.

As a final effort, negotiate within the limits authorized and based on a trade-off of some description.

To overcome objections about your product, demonstrate and describe, with emphasis on the features that nullify the objection.

Try for a trial order.

Bring the skeptical prospects to your plant and show them how you do it.

Service

Closely allied to complaints about price and product are those related to service. It is of no value to a customer that your product is the best that he or she can buy at a competitive price unless you can deliver the goods to fully meet the needs.

But in this case there is one basic difference. If the product is good and the price is right, it is almost inexcusable to lose the order. Again you must find the basis for the objection and attack that.

This was a very special problem for us during a change from a manual to a computer system for order entry and processing. The situation was horrendous for a few months and we lost lots of business and even some old customers. They were sympathetic (some of them had even gone through the same experience), but they placed their orders elsewhere. When things did finally straighten out, we were confronted with a massive job to regain the lost ground.

We staged a major campaign. We assembled all of the data the computer processing afforded concerning the filling and shipping of orders—time required to enter and process, time required to complete the orders and ship them, ratios of shipped items to those back-ordered, and time to complete the back orders. We had a status report daily and made week-to-week and month-to-month comparisons to highlight our progress.

Then we invited our former customers and the most skeptical of those who had stayed with us to the plant for a planned presentation of how we had improved and what we could do once the bugs had been eliminated. Those whom we could not bring in were given the story in their offices with the aid of an organized presentation. Gradually, we regained most of the lost business and with the same ammunition attracted several new customers.

Granted, everyone does not have such a problem every day, but the things we did to solve it will work every day. The chief need of anyone who complains about your service is reassurance. You need to restore confidence that you are reliable. Give the prospect information that will convince him or her that you can perform, if not in the detail we did to solve a big problem, then sufficiently to dispel minor doubts.

For this one, too, letters and comments from other customers will help. Tell the prospect about those whom you have helped in emergencies and by expediting shipments before the originally scheduled dates. Call those customers and let them tell your prospect.

There is one particularly opportune time to sell a customer who questions your service capability. When you have a special marketing program, as most companies often do, use the incentive to get a trial order from recalcitrant prospects. It will give you an opportunity to show how good your service can be.

Remember This

The poorest reason of all to lose a good order is unsatisfactory service.

Your superiors agree on that. Feeling somewhat guilty, they will help you as much as possible. Enlist their special help and together devise some means to get that trial order.

Then ensure that you perform.

Company

Complaints of a general nature about companies are usually based on false or insufficient information. That incorrect knowledge must be corrected.

Most companies have excellent sales aids showing how they started several years before in a ramshackle building and how, through the years, they have become a significant factor in their industry. That is probably your story, too. Tell it again and again. Use all of the aids you have and embellish the story with verifiable current successes.

Show your prospects facts and figures depicting your growth. Use financial statements, sales graphs, or whatever you have that colors your company successful and aggressive.

We used to have a weekly production schedule. It listed every job in the plant by customer name, with other important details about each—value of the order, date of entry, date required for shipment, and other dates showing schedule and completion in various departments. It was really an internal aid to help our people check progress of all orders and to form the basis for a weekly evaluation of where we stood on each job in the plant.

It was not intended for public display and that very reason made it one of my useful sales tools. Its rough, dittoed form made it look like an instrument for confidential use, giving it an authenticity that is sometimes lacking in a slick, polished piece by the advertising agency. It was revised weekly and, as a result, was always current.

I carried two or three of these of different dates to cover the typical progress of a big job that might be in production for as much as six months. I used them in several ways. Sometimes it was necessary only to show the names of the major, national companies for whom we had substantial orders. It was always gratifying to see the surprise on the faces of the prospects when one schedule might have more than one job each for several blue chip companies.

On other occasions, I reviewed the status on several of the jobs to indicate that we were right on schedule, or ahead. If we happened to be behind, the reasons which were spelled out in a special column showed that they usually were beyond our control.

This form rarely failed to get attention. It seemed immediately reliable and it was never seriously questioned or maligned.

During your travels, observe how many companies with lousy reputations for product, service, and corporate image are sending out traveling salespersons every day and consider how many orders they must be getting just to stay in business. Take pride in your company and how much it can offer, and do not lose any orders because of objections about the things that really make you superior.

Remember This

There is a story behind every company that is successful in today's marketplace, yours included.

When an objection applies to your company, tell your story, over and over, and close more orders, over and over.

Indecision, Inertia, and Delay

The other three common objections are less tangible and possibly not as well based. They may be all the more subtle and difficult to handle. As for all objections, the greatest help lies in knowing the real objection and its basis. In general terms, that must boil down to finding some inducement for the prospect to buy now, not later.

A sensible first approach is to recite the advantages of ordering immediately—assured delivery on time, hedge against price increases, completion of purchase details so that other problems may be tackled, immediate benefit from the use of the new products or equipment, elimination of future shortage or delay, and anything else your imagination and knowledge of forecasts can suggest.

There are always current events to provide closing aids to salespeople. In good times, material shortages or procurement delays threaten delivery. They make things hard to get. Describe the conditions that way—"hard to get"—because buyers become more eager when things are "hard to get."

Use your own backlog situation as reason to place the order now so that you can get it into your production schedule immediately. Tell your prospect how others are doing that very thing.

Even during less prosperous times, when most are reluctant to spend money, there are built-in stimuli. Depressions cannot last forever, and there are always respected economists predicting an early turnabout. Convince your prospect that he or she cannot afford to wait until that happens before placing the order. There will be lots of orders then, full production schedules, and manufacturing and shipping delays. There will also be much greater chances that higher prices will prevail.

In a depression, your prospect's sales must be off, too. Some forward-thinking buyers are most receptive to expansion at such times as the only means of decreasing their costs or gaining a bigger market share.

For adverse times, your company might offer reduced prices, extended credit, or some such concession to stimulate business. Make the best of those special aids. Mention them in every case where the customer is sold but will not make the move to buy.

If the particular concessions you have been authorized do not work, find out what would be more attractive and suggest that to your superiors. Check and report what your competitors are doing. Instead of complaining that you do not have what you need to make sales, use your imagination to suggest what might work. Your superiors need your input and will welcome some new ideas if they make sense.

If the delay appears to be a personal hesitancy on the part of the prospect, you might want to "talk around" him or her. In your discussion, describe the needs and benefits in terms of the company rather than the individual. Try to develop the fear that delay might work hardship on the company for which he or she will surely have to shoulder the ultimate blame. Use some phrases like these: "You know your company needs this, Jack"; or "Consider the benefit to your company if you buy now." Maybe this will do it: "You wouldn't want your company to have trouble getting this on time, would you?" or "If you wait too long, this will surely cost your company more money."

Sometimes a buyer delays because he or she really does not have the authority to finally commit to the purchase but is too proud to admit it. Without further wounding that pride, you should offer to help to convince others. Some sympathetic statement like this might help: "You know you need to buy this now, Jack. Is there anyone I can help you convince? If this costs more later, you will be the one to be criticized."

If all else fails, ask your prospect what it would take to get the order today. Caution that any order with exceptions might not be accepted but that you will submit a reasonable proposition to your boss. Then negotiate the best deal you can and permit the customer to note the provisions on the face of the purchase order. Special plant conditions might make it attractive.

Even if the order is not accepted as submitted, it does represent a tentative commitment and places you in a position for further bargaining. It also forces the buyer to check with his or her higher authority if that was the problem, and the buyer can show that he or she did gain something for the company.

You should not use this technique for products for which firm prices are published unless there are unusual quantities or some other variation from normal. It might be illegal, and such tactics could undermine a price structure. This applies more to specialized machinery that is bid on an individual basis.

Remember This

In good times or bad, there are always plenty of reasons to delay, but there are always more for doing something now.

If you sell a customer on a product but fail to get the order, you might be doing all the hard work for your next competitor who comes by.

ANTICIPATING OBJECTIONS

The most effective aid to overcoming objections is to anticipate them in advance. At least two important benefits may be gained:

1. You can assemble all data and any other requirements and refine your refutation in advance.

2. When you are confident an objection will be raised, you can introduce it first. That establishes immediate credibility because no buyer would believe that you would suggest something that might jeopardize your sale unless you had utmost confidence that it was not really objectionable.

To the inexperienced salesperson, it might seem to be a difficult job even to overcome objections, let alone figure out what they will be beforehand. Obviously, cleverness and confidence in this area are built best by experience, but as a start, it is helpful to know where the lessons are. These are some of the clues to possible objections:

1. What other prospects and customers have said.
2. How this prospect has responded to your discussion, and the questions asked.
3. How you predict this prospect will react, based on your gaining an intimate acquaintance with your prospects.

What Others Have Said

Every fruitful sales presentation should evoke some comment or question from the listener. Ask questions that will stimulate response, give him or her time to react, and then listen to what is said.

From day *one* of your sales career, you should be tuned in for objections. Once you have heard one, study your product and your company until you can refute it.

When it is clear that you are not going to make a sale, discuss in detail every possible objection the prospect might have. Use the session for your education, and belabor each point more fully than you might in a normal sales discussion when you might want to avoid exaggerating the objections. What you can learn might help you later.

How Your Prospect Has Responded

In all sales discussions, get your prospect into the act; let him or her show you what you need to know. The correct word is "show" because you need to do more than just listen. Note the prospect's spontaneous reaction to all you say. Measure his or her intensity and be alert to any sign of the importance placed on any remark. Note how long each point is discussed and how many times it is mentioned. Think about what the prospect says and be alert for the emotions that are displayed as each observation is made.

Sort out the objections the prospect raises and compare them with those you have mentally cataloged from previous experiences. Consider how these might be similar to what others have said and how your solutions to other objections might help you in this instance.

Intimate Acquaintance
with Your Prospect

Very little of the sales conversation between a salesperson and a prospect should be purposeless. Neither the prospect nor you have much time for that. Inconsequential ice breakers might serve a purpose, but the thinking salesperson, the real pro, has a reason for all remarks and questions.

Try to learn all you can about all of your prospects—how they react, what they think, how truthfully and accurately they express what they think, their personalities, their temperaments, their integrity, their ethical and moral values, their concerns and lifestyles, their goals, their responsibilities, their likes and dislikes, and their fortes and foibles.

You really need to know what makes them tick. You need to know and understand characters because most of what all of us think, do, and say is almost always in character.

I have always found it helpful to know something about a stranger before I called on him or her. When I was riding down the highway with a salesman to call on someone he knew but I did not, I used to ask him all I could about the person we were going to see. If nothing more, it gave me some idea of what we might encounter and made me feel better prepared and more at ease and more confident.

Personal conversations in the office are helpful if there is a plan. To the extent that personal matters help, discuss them. Let your prospects tell you about themselves and stimulate conversation with your personal revelations.

Make a total effort to know all you can about the really important prospects. Ask others about them. Observe them at every opportunity. Get acquainted with them as you would a friend or neighbor. Those whom you know best will surprise you least even when it comes to the objections they might raise to buying your products.

A PRACTICAL CONSIDERATION

This might sound like defeatism, but I prefer to think it is pragmatism. If you have done your very best and, in your opinion, all objections have been fairly overruled yet all you can get from your prospect is a grunt or two, give it up. Pack up your briefcase and head down the road to the next prospect. Do not be hard-headed at the expense of wasted time. That is like an NFL football team, down by twenty points, using all of their time-outs in the last minute of play.

BE A PRO

Constantly prepare for objections. They can kill an order but, once over-come, they can pave the way for a rapid close. Study your product on a continuing basis, noting especially the design features that overcome the objections you hear. Cultivate your top production person and tour the plant with him or her regularly to keep fully abreast of new machines and new manufacturing methods. The more you know about your product and its manufacture, the better you are prepared to meet objections—those you anticipate and the unexpected ones, too.

Make yourself an authority on your competitors' products. The confidence that having that knowledge will give you will help overcome objections and dominate your sales presentations.

Anticipate objections. Mentally catalog all you ever hear and file the answers right alongside them. Be alert for possible objections as you proceed through each sales presentation.

When an objection is raised, analyze it. Ask questions. Pay strict attention to the answers. When you know what the exact objection is, meet it head-on.

There is a certain finality to the statement by the judge during a court action, "Objection overruled." And the decision is normally rendered quickly. Do the same when you hear an objection. Overrule it fast. Do not belabor or glorify it.

And remember—if a prospect voices an objection, he or she has some interest in your product. It cannot be emphasized too strongly that the objection is also one of the loudest buying signals you can be given.

Sometimes even when you are satisfied that you have done your best in replying to an objection, you might sense that you still have not made the sale. Ask for the order anyway. Maybe your prospect was more convinced than you thought. Or maybe you will get lucky; everyone does at one time or another.

chapter six

Closing the sale

*Closing the sale is all important;
there are no silver or bronze
medals for sales achievement—only gold*

INTRODUCTION

The effectiveness of all sales efforts is dependent upon the closing of the sale. Unless an order is the final result, all preparations and presentations are worthless except for any experience they might afford. Closing techniques merit serious study and diligent practice.

Closing elements are so integral to the entire selling effort that they should not be isolated. Regardless of the stage of progress, a salesperson should never overlook an opportunity to move in and close a sale. Whether it is a discussion with just a lone buyer or an elaborate production for a large group, the effort to sell something begins just as soon as a prospect's need and intention to buy are indicated.

TRIAL CLOSING

One of the skills most important to a salesperson's success is the ability to discern when a buyer is ready to buy. In a presentation, a skillful salesperson is constantly sending up trial balloons to measure the possibility of making the sale. This practice is called *trial closing*.

To me, trial closing is an effort which, if it fails, will not terminate the interview or end a salesperson's chance for the order later in the discussion. It is not in any respect just a "try" or half-hearted attempt. It is a trial in the sense of being a test of the progress toward finalizing the sale. It is an effort to determine how nearly sold the prospect is and what else must be done.

Sometimes all it takes to get the order is just one trial closing attempt. When that happens to you, pass your pen to the prospect with something to sign, a proposal or contract, or an order. Forget that long sales exposition you have so diligently prepared and say nothing more than you must to clear all of the details. Do not talk yourself out of the sale.

Unfortunately, it is not that simple in most cases. It is not always easy to recognize the closing signals and, more often than not, they must be sensed as much as heard. A salesperson must continually be alert to his or her progress, and there are subtle signals that it might be just the right time to ask for the order. Choosing the proper time to ask for it is a big factor in success.

Here are some of the cues that could help you:

1. Any persistence of the customer to clarify or satisfy himself or herself on a particular detail, especially if all other points appear to be acceptable.
2. Repeated agreement with you as you make your sales points as indicated by verbal assent, nod of approval, or accord with what you say.
3. Any heightened interest in the product or any hint that the need is urgent.
4. All questions about price, availability, and delivery.
5. Any interest about such things as warranty, service after the sale, repair parts availability, and so on.
6. Any suggestion that the prospect has heard all that is necessary to make a decision.

7. Anything that gives you the feeling that you have convinced the prospect that you have what he or she needs and wants.

8. The most unexpected of all to some salespersons, an objection, as discussed in more detail in Chapter Five.

If a prospect is totally noncommital, giving no buying signals, asking questions is the principal means of gaining information. The questions need to be carefully phrased, based on your discussion. Try to use questions that will elicit affirmative responses; it is unwise to reinforce negative replies at any point.

Naturally, you should attempt to close immediately if any answer gives a clear signal that the prospect is ready to buy.

Here are some sample questions:

"How does that sound, OK?"
"Does that answer your question?"
"This is just what you need, isn't it?
"Have you decided on the accessories?"
"When will you want this in your plant?"
"How do you want it shipped?"
"Do you want partials or one complete shipment?"

Once you have established a pattern of agreement, your questions should be designed for further commitment. In no case should you ask a question that might prompt a firm decline early in your questioning. Save those questions requiring a really committed reply until you are satisfied that the prospect is sold.

Remember This

In a sales presentation, do not just wait until the prospect says, "I want that."

Tell the prospect and show why he or she needs it, and while you are doing that, be alert for the signals that tell you that you may ask, "What is your order number?"

MY TOP CLOSING TECHNIQUES

Somewhere along the line, you will sense that all obstacles have been over-come and that the sale could now be made. That is the moment when the winners are separated from the losers. The skilled salesperson comes out with the order. The less able leave later, empty-handed, without really knowing how close they came.

All experienced and successful salespersons have their repertoire of closing techniques. Those that have worked best and most often for me and for others I know can be readily summarized.

1. The Classic Close

The most satisfying accomplishment in closing an order is the one that develops during a thoroughly planned and well-executed sales presenta-tion. It signifies that the effort has covered exactly what was required to allay all of the prospect's fears, remove all doubts, and overcome all objec-tions. Somewhere along the line, the prospect has decided that this is what he or she wants, and there is no need for further delay. The prospect has been sold and is eager to buy.

A good salesperson knows when this point has come and does not belabor the subjects that have been accepted, thus risking a chance to sug-gest new doubts and talk the prospect out of placing an order. This sales-person proceeds to details of shipment and other terms and conditions, with no indication of doubt about the order. Once these minor details have been cleared, the professional salesperson presents the contract for signature or simply asks, "What is your order number, Mr. Jones?"

During such a close, there has been no need to ask with an awkward feeling, "May I have this order, Mr. Jones?" All doubt about that has been eliminated, and Mr. Jones does not need to think about actually placing the order or to agonize over the decision. He has been gradually led to the point where it seems the only logical action left.

This is truly the classic close. It is almost automatic and results when a skilled salesperson has so thoroughly planned and executed the sale that success has been ensured from the start.

The first time this ever happened to me was in El Paso, Texas. My boss came down from Dayton, Ohio, to help me sell a prospective distribu-tor in an area where we greatly needed coverage. We had been wooing this prospect for four to six months, and this was our chance to make the climaxing presentation. We were to meet with all key personnel of the distributor. Three days were devoted to the preparation for the meeting, and I learned what planning and preparation were all about.

During the meeting, I learned what execution was all about. We shared the presentation, but that boss from Dayton took care of the last third of the meeting and he led them into total agreement with our program. What we could do that could help them was emphasized and made to appear irresistible to all of the prospect's personnel. They were first to start saying, "We can do this with your line . . . . " or "That will solve our problem at XYZ Company."

At the point of their highest enthusiasm for the joint marketing plans we discussed for the area, my teacher brought out the prepared contract, went over it, and presented it to the general manager. He took a vote aloud with a simple question, "This is what you want isn't it, fellas?" and started reading the contract while they nodded in assent. Within ten minutes the signature was added.

This impressed me so much at that stage of my experience that I was afraid it was almost too high-pressured. I lost all doubt about that during the following months when this association proved so profitable for both of us. That had not been a slick sales success. Everything had been true, and it had worked out just as had been foretold by a professional salesperson.

2. The Pressure Pause

Sometimes the most articulate closing stroke is complete silence. Assume that you have finished your presentation. You have answered all questions, stressed all of your product's features, overcome objections and covered all of the reasons to buy. Your prospect has indicated that he has no more questions and you have nothing more to say.

When you reach this point and momentary silence follows, say nothing. Let the silence develop. Sit absolutely still and present to the prospect an image that says, "There is nothing more to say. Now it is up to you. Just give me the order." This forces this prospect to make the decision without your bugging him or her to do so. And the prospect has very limited choices. He or she can object but has already raised all possible objections and they have been answered. Or the prospect can say no, or just procrastinate. But his or her need and approval of your product have already been indicated. The longer the prospect thinks about it without interruption, the more convinced he or she will be that there is only one thing to do—give you the order.

If you speak first, you will remove all pressure from the prospect and make it easy for him or her to offer some feeble excuse, such as, "I guess I'd better wait a day or two," or "Maybe I'd better check and see if John still agrees with this."

One day I was working with a distributor salesman, and as we were driving between calls, we discussed this technique. A chance to try it came up on the very next call. We had shown a special drive unit to a cotton gin manager for one of his cleaning machines. After we had explained all of the features, he asked a few questions, raised one objection that we convinced him would cause no problem, and seemed to run out of anything more to say.

My companion and I were able to exchange a nod and both of us remained silent. I began to think it was becoming a little embarrassing, but we held our silence. We had hoped to sell one of the drive packages, so we were really surprised when the cotton gin manager broke the silence with, "I'll take two of those drives."

3. Extra Incentive

Some prospects are obviously sold on your product or service, yet they simply will not give you the order. They are procrastinators but only because of an aversion to making decisions. Once you have sold someone, you must get the order. Unless you get it immediately, the chances are good that you might lose it, and very possibly to the very next salesperson who comes in offering the same thing. Such an outcome indicates that you did all of the work but failed to collect the reward.

Try an extra incentive when you encounter this standoff. If it is a concession in price that you offer, be careful how you do that or your prospect will wonder why you did not make the lower price available in the first place.

One occasion when it worked for me stands out in my memory. A reluctant buyer would not make any commitment, yet he was positive about his intention to buy and averred that our product was acceptable. I asked if I could call the office before he decided definitely to delay the order. I told him I wanted to check our delivery once more.

During the call, I learned that a job we had already scheduled for production had been delayed because of trouble in completing the customer's building. This would justify a slight reduction in price for an order that could be fitted into the void in the production schedule.

My prospect had been concerned about delivery and his requirements could be worked into our revised schedule with some benefit. The slight concession in price and the chance that delivery could be improved were enough to get the order that day. To make the report of my call to the office seem genuine, I showed the prospect the job on the production schedule (of which I always carried several copies) that had been unexpectedly moved back to a later date.

You can often help yourself by considering possible concessions for such an impasse. In your initial planning, provide an ace in the hole for such a contingency, but do not offer it until you are confident that no other stumbling block can possibly exist. Once a concession has been made, it is hard to withdraw it later, even if the reason for its original justification no longer exists. There is also the danger that one concession freely given will cause wonder about how much more reduction can be obtained.

4. Fear

Some tactics are not considered entirely fair and ethical, but on many occasions real events provide justification for mentioning potential problems that could delay a shipment. A threatened strike, a material shortage, an imminent price increase, and other possibilities can be major concerns for a prospective buyer if delivery can be affected. You owe it to the prospect to explain the possibilities and inform him or her of the chance of delayed shipment.

Your own workload can be a factor, too. Tell the prospect when it is excessive and urge him or her to get into the schedule. There are two appeals in this consideration. First, the fact that you are busy will enhance the image of your company. Poorly qualified manufacturers have more slack periods than the good ones. And secondly, when a prospect expects that something will be hard to get, the need becomes more acute.

5. The Repeat Attempt

When a closing effort fails, it should be considered another opportunity rather than a failure. It affords an excellent chance to find out what really is required to get the order because when fair-minded persons say "no," they feel some compulsion to give a reason. The order is not irrevocably lost until it has been given to someone else.

Your follow up is a simple question—"Why?" If you have just been told you will not get the order, you might be inclined to ask the question gruffly or even belligerently. Avoid that. Ask as sympathetically as you can. Show surprise that you are not to get the order and let your questioning indicate that you feel that all of the advantages have not been understood.

Keep asking "Why?" until you find out exactly what the reason is. Review your sales story as necessary. Take encouragement that you might know what the real problem is for the first time. Especially if your prospect is cooperative and shows no impatience, you might still have a chance.

Ask for time to assemble additional facts. As you do that, enlist more help for your next discussion with the prospect. Finally give up only after you are satisfied that you have done your best and then do so gracefully. There will be other days and other orders. It would be unwise to lose a customer as well as the order.

In the early 1950s, the farmers of west Texas were converting the power source for their irrigation wells to natural gas. Those with neighboring land formed groups and installed plastic pipe gas lines from the main line to their wells. For a while the business was booming. It was also very competitive.

After the groups had been formed, they would meet, make their plans, and call in the designers and bidders for the line. They would then vote to reach their final decisions.

I had a friend who sold plastic pipe. He was a very skillful salesman and thorough in all of his efforts. He customarily became acquainted with every member of each prospective group and convinced all of them that they needed his pipe. By the time of the final vote, he knew where he stood with each member.

On one particular line he was sure that he had cinched the pipe order. But in the final meeting it was voted to install a competitive brand. My friend could not accept that. That night and the next day, he met individually with each group member, repeating the benefits that they had previously accepted. They met again and he got the order.

That showed me that a salesperson should not give up easily. Few orders might be saved like that, but some have been. And that proves that all is not lost if the first verdict is against you, especially if you are still in session with the voters.

6. High-Pressure Close

There is a technique that I would be reluctant to include if it had not worked for me. Prepare in advance of a special meeting something for the prospect to sign (this is always good practice). After you have answered all of the questions, have eliminated all objections, and have received nod after nod in agreement but are still given excuses, pass the prepared instrument to your prospect and hand him or her a pen. Urge the prospect, "Come on, Mr. Jones, you know you want this. Just go ahead and sign the contract."

At first thought, this seems so brazen that it should insult the intelligence of the prospect. If used on the correct one, it does not. Some people have always been told what to do and the extra urging is unconsciously appreciated.

The first time it worked for me, I said it half in jest, and two-thirds of the way in doubt that it would work. I half chuckled as I did it, but to my surprise, the prospect seemed relieved that his decision making had been shared to some extent. Or maybe his grin, as he signed the contract, indicated that he had done the same thing himself.

Sometime when you have a similar prospect in such a situation and you can think of no other way to proceed, try it. Your chances will be improved if you have given some preliminary thought to the choice of your prospect for this technique.

7. The Yes Nod

The rhetoricians undoubtedly deserve credit for inspiring this one. They are often called upon to prepare a discourse to persuade an audience and frequently that audience is considered hostile, or ostensibly not in sympathy with the views of the writer or speaker. They have a special technique for this requirement which they call the YES NOD, or the YES-YES model.

What is rhetoric, in this instance, but a form of selling? It is certainly similar enough that it is only natural that the rhetorical method should be adaptable to the closing of sales.

The theory suggests to the salesperson that a pattern be established of YES responses to questions for which the obvious answers would be yes. Then when that tendency toward the affirmative replies is strongly established, ask more vital questions for which the yes would imply commitment.

The questions should be posed after you have finished your discussion of all of the advantages of your product as your final wrap-up and closing effort. The series of questions could develop like this for someone selling machine lubricating oils:

"Mr. Jones, you would like to decrease machine down time, wouldn't you?"

He can hardly say no to that.

"And save money at the same time?"

That one, too, should get Mr. Jones' sincere and prompt concurrence.

After other questions relevant to points covered in your discussion, your clincher could be something like this:

"Since you want all of the benefits our product will offer, you surely want to buy some of our lubricants, don't you?" or "With all of that to gain, you certainly want to try some of our products on your machines, right, Mr. Jones?"

8. Ask for the Order

One of the simplest and most straightforward closing techniques that should be used most frequently is often the most neglected. It is the plain request for an order. When a salesperson calls on a purchasing agent or buyer, he or she has only one reason—to sell something, to get an order. Yet I have worked with innumerable salespeople who became so deeply involved in the conversation that we actually left without any request for an order.

Try this some time when you run out of other things to say. You should never leave a purchasing department without asking for an order. Even if you are working on something that cannot possibly be finalized for several weeks, there are other needs in the meantime. Ask for something. After all, you do not want anyone to lose sight of your principal objective, even while you sweat out the big sale.

Sometimes the earlier you ask, the better you fare. We once had a customer to whom we had sold a lot of equipment. But then for a reason we could not discover, we stopped getting the orders even though we quoted as we always had.

A new purchasing agent was hired and contacted us to bid a substantial job. We explained that, based on our recent experience with them, it was doubtful that we could afford the time to work up the quotation, busy as we were.

The purchasing agent called back and we ultimately told him we would bid the requirements, but that our purpose would be to sell them the equipment, not merely furnish a bid for purposes of comparison. We were assured that we could meet with their key people to discuss our bid after it had been reviewed.

Two weeks later the district manager and I went to Piqua, Ohio, to hold that meeting. When we asked the receptionist for the purchasing agent, she replied (with the apparent glee they sometimes exhibit when there is no one for a salesperson to see) that he had been called out of town. I could almost hear the district manager thinking, "I knew it." But by that time, she had got around to reading our cards.

"Oh, you gentlemen are with ABC Company. Mr. _____ (the purchasing agent) scheduled a meeting for you before he left."

After assembling with several engineers and completing the introductions and small talk, there was a pause and the leader of their group asked what we had in mind. Since we were expecting them to have all of the questions, it caught us a little off guard. All I could say was, "Well, sir, we're here to finalize the details of your order for the Mexican job."

His immediate reply was, "We're going to give you that order today, but we do need to clear a few details."

The district manager was sitting next to me, and out of the corner of my eye, I caught his spontaneous twitch as he braced himself to keep from falling out of his chair.

We had asked for this order at least twice. We had virtually asked for it before we agreed to bid. And we had opened our remarks by asking again. True, we did spend the rest of the day discussing options and details, but even then I was never involved in as big a sale that was committed as rapidly as that one. And I must admit, I was not totally candid about how easy it was when I got back to the office.

9. Sustained Purchase

There is one closing technique that is built into the receipt of any order. It is based on the premise that once a buyer has ordered something, it becomes much easier to sell him or her something else while he or she is still in the buying mood. Old timers will recall the days when special items were given emphasis as "order starters." They were featured as special bargains in some way for the very purpose of starting a purchase, which could then be expanded into a larger order. Even today few good clothing salespersons will stop after you have bought a suit. They will say, "How about a sport coat and slacks to alternate with that?" The least they will do is suggest a shirt and tie to complete the outfit.

The lesson is that once the buy decision has been made, a big obstacle has been overcome. You have accessory or complementary items that you could suggest anytime you make a sale. Remember that increasing an order is just as good as making a new sale and usually much easier.

This worked so well for me one time that it nearly put me in a box. In a given city, I had two distributors. Each of them had salespersons who called on many of the same accounts and as always in such a situation, there was a certain amount of juggling to do. For the most part, it was possible to keep everybody happy. Most of the customers looked to one of the distributors for some needs and to the other for other products. There were usually projects working with both but not normally the same ones.

Both of the salespeople in one area and I had discussed sales techniques, and we made a game out of our work together trying to sell more each day.

One day, Joe from A company and I were calling on XYZ Company, which had prospective orders working with both of the competing distributor salespeople. Early in our conversation it became clear that the XYZ buyer was ready to buy the equipment about which he had been talking to Joe and me. That order was so easy that Joe was not ready to give up. He asked, "What else are you going to need for the new cotton harvest?"

The response was, "Aw well, I might as well give you the whole works." And he did, including all of the things he had discussed with Jake from B company and me. As a result, we went out of there with a really good order and there was little chance that any other sales would be made in the foreseeable future, except for breakdowns during the cotton harvesting season. For the first time ever, I had an order I would have preferred to be a little smaller.

Two weeks later I was due to work with Jake. I had not yet decided how to handle the problem that was sure to come up. It did, the minute I walked into B company and met Jake. He said nothing—not good morning, how are you, or anything as he usually would.

I greeted him, and finally he said, "I can't work with you today. Go spend the day with Joe."

Fortunately, he was a fine fellow and agreed to go get a cup of coffee. He couldn't resist that because those were the early days of coffee popularity when hardly anyone could refuse a cup early in the day before anything stronger sounded good. During that time, I drank so much coffee that I knew that if I ever had an obstruction of a vital, internal organ, it would be caused by coffee beans floating in a muddy liquid.

After that first cup, Jake felt better and simmered down. When I told him that I knew what was bugging him and did not blame him a bit, he became more congenial. "You know how much we have talked about getting all you can every time you start an order," I said and added, "They were ready to buy. I'm sorry it worked out that way."

Jake said, "Aw, you SOB, let's get to work. I know where there are a couple of orders, and one of them might be Joe's." After that fond term, SOB, I knew all was OK.

My biggest surprise was the ease with which Jake took the explanation on hearing the reason that Joe had to get all he could once he started. He understood that.

10. Last Objection

It is emphasized throughout this book that objections are really signals to close a sale. It is normally thought that this applies to a major objection that must be resolved before a sale can be made. Actually the same is true of minor objections.

In fact, if a minor objection is refuted in a spectacular fashion, it can sometimes push a major objection, one more difficult to handle, into the background. It might then be possible to close the sale without ever really resolving what seemed to be the more important objection. Some think of this as a separate closing technique and tag it, "Closing on a minor objection."

For the LAST OBJECTION technique, either a major or minor objection can provide the starting point.

After many objections have been overcome, you will reach what appears to be the last one. Before you answer it, ask if there are any other objections. If the answer is "no," repeat the question for ensuring and emphasizing that there are no more.

Confirm that, "Now all of you are sure that there are no more objections, right?"

When the statement is reconfirmed, go on, "Well, if there are no more than this one objection, then it seems to me that you will be ready to sign the order, provided I can satisfy this last objection. Is that right?"

It is unlikely that anyone could disagree with that assumption. Just go on and solve the objection and make the sale.

This can be polished even beyond what was just suggested. You could select the objection you want to be that last critical one from those that have come up before. Then you could choose one for which you knew you had a very convincing solution. That is easy to do. When an objection is raised and you know you have overwhelming evidence that it is not valid, merely say, "Let me hold that one and I'll get to it later." Then make that your last objection and tie in an order commitment as outlined in the preceding paragraph.

I had a very unusual experience with this, one time. I was on an airplane to Phoenix, Arizona, where the district sales manager and I were to make a formal presentation to a large and much-wanted, multibranch distributor we had been trying to close for some time.

We had prepared, as thoroughly as we knew how, to meet with a group of some eighteen to twenty of the top persons of the organization—those who made the important decisions. Our presentation was to be given during one of their special planning sessions for which they periodically convened.

When I finished going over my notes one last time on the plane, I pulled a trade journal out of my briefcase for a few minutes' diversion before landing. As I thumbed through it, I came to a short article headed, "Closing Technique for the Month," or something like that. The article suggested what I have outlined in the preceding paragraphs.

I thought about that and then reviewed my notes about the objections that we had anticipated might come up. I sorted out one or two for which we had the most convincing arguments.

During the meeting, one of these objections was raised and I was able to delay it as the last to be covered. Later, all agreed that it was the last objection and that if it were satisfied, we had a deal. It worked exactly as the writer of that short feature article had suggested it would. No other closing technique was needed, and the contract was signed. It was surprisingly simple because some of our close contacts in the organization had told us we might have difficulty in selling all of those present.

11. Summary of Objections vs. Benefits

One day one of our field salespeople called to tell me about an order he had just sold. Since it was to a tough, old prospect, I asked him how he had done it. He had been calling on this hard-to-get person for months but had never received anything but unimportant objections. He had constantly offered offsetting advantages, but they had never seemed to register with the prospect.

He finally made the sale by the simple expedient of summarizing all of the objections and all of the advantages on a sheet of paper, the former in a small area at the top and the latter spread all over the rest of the sheet. When the prospect noted the obvious imbalance of his objections to the advantages available to him, his resistance immediately collapsed. Indeed, he appeared to feel guilty that he had failed to act before.

We have all summarized objections and strong points, but it was the written summary that did the trick. The inescapable conclusion became too obvious when reduced to writing.

CONCLUSION

Psychologists say that one can seldom change the mind of another. The best that can be expected is that something might be said or done to influence the decision of that other person.

There is a lesson in that maxim for all persons in sales. They should strive to help buyers to decide to buy from them. The buyers should be drawn into the closing effort as much as possible. Their imaginations should be stimulated to the extent that they can visualize owning what the salespersons have to offer.

Closing techniques are not gimmicks or tricks and there probably is not any single one that is fail-safe. An effective summary of your strongest, best-accepted points and the proper choice of closing techniques to meet the conditions are the most important requirements. The closing part of your exercise should be your best prepared and most rehearsed.

Some closing techniques will be more productive than others in certain situations. You should have alternate methods for closing well in mind for all major presentations. If you lose during the close, you lose all.

BE A PRO

Cultivate expertise in closing sales. That is what selling is all about.

For every prospective sale, have several closing techniques in mind. Outline them and be ready to employ them as effectively as you know how. Then as you proceed through your presentation, decide which of your choices should be most applicable.

Ask for the order at every opportunity. You do not have to compartmentalize your effort and ask for the order only during the closing segment. Ask for it again and again.

Profit from every closing effort. Close the sale first and then learn from each experience, even those that do not succeed.

There are myriad so-called closing techniques. As your experience increases, develop and refine your own methods. Adapt your closing moves to what makes you comfortable and to what enables you to make sales.

chapter seven

Follow-up calls

*Any sales call that creates any interest in the prospect
merits a follow-up call.*

THE FOLLOW-UP NATURE OF CALLS

Calls have figured very prominently in all subject matter thus far—how to
plan them, how to prepare for them, and how to execute them. But there
is one aspect of most calls that is unique and that has not received sufficient emphasis in merely general treatment.

That relates to the follow-up element in most calls. Unless you are
making your first call on a prospect or just dropping into a buyer's office
to see if you can sell anything, most calls follow up something. You are
working on a prospect who needs further cultivating; or you are pursuing
an order for a major plant expansion; or in the case of distributors, there
are frequent follow-up calls for training and general assistance in your
cooperative efforts to increase sales.

SYSTEM FOR FOLLOW-UP

The follow-up nature of so many calls suggests that a system should be devised to make certain that all unfinished business is handled promptly, so that a continuity may be maintained in a continuing sales effort. The latter should eliminate the need to start each new call with, "What did we talk about last time?" or "Where do we stand on this?"

To me, the one who does best in following up on previous calls is the most professional of all professionals, the doctor. I used to see one periodically for a condition that was not too serious, and I was always impressed at how rapidly and smoothly he got into the business at hand on each of my visits.

First, I was ushered into a cubicle where a nurse checked the routine things—weight, blood pressure, pulse, and so on. She always had a file with her and made notes of her findings in that file.

Sooner or later (most often later), the doctor came in, and he was reading that file as he entered. He would say, "Hello. How are you feeling?" and get right to work thumping my chest and listening on his stethoscope. He always seemed to know what my condition had been last time and soon had all of his answers on the current status. He would then suggest I put my shirt back on and come into his office.

When I got there, he was reading past notes in the file and making new ones. He gave me a report, perhaps wrote a prescription, cautioned me not to do this or that, recommended that I do something else, and said he would see me in three months.

As I left, he picked up another file and headed for another cubicle. I could not help feeling that he would display the same intimate knowledge and the same dispatch that he had with me even though that patient's problem might be far different from mine.

His all-business attitude intrigued me, and I could not help wondering how anyone could appear so much in control of the situation. As I drove home, I finally realized what made it possible for him to seem so fully informed about my health as if I were his only patient. It was that file, and even though I had been going to him for several years, it was not a bulging, unmanageable mess.

That suggested to me a follow-up system that worked. There are endless possibilities. I know that because I had tried and discarded many of them. For my ultimate plan, I adopted a folder something like the doctor's. Mine was a plain manila file folder. I set one up for each major account and another one for the smaller miscellaneous ones.

On the inside of the front, I wrote the name, address (including shipping address, if different), telephone number, telex number, and any special instructions for mailing or shipping. Below that I listed all of the personnel I knew with titles and a note about their responsibilities. I tried to include a brief comment on anything special about the person or his or her job. I did not include birthday, spouse's name, favorite color, or any of the other details some salespersons keep up with so well. I just was not ready for such embellishments.

I made a maximum effort to ensure that names and titles were correct. The best source was business cards, and I had a sizable file of those. I still have it.

On the other cover of the folder, I placed several lined sheets from an ordinary yellow scratch pad under an Acco fastener. I took notes during each call and then summarized them briefly on the lined pages, showing date, persons visited, subjects discussed, orders taken, orders or other matters pending, and suggestions about what needed follow-up next time, with a big X in the margin to indicate the most urgent items. Whenever I had time, I entered these notes before I left the premises.

I put into the file any papers I accumulated that pertained to the pending or unfinished business, including the following:

1. Notes on all orders pending.
2. Commitments for future work with distributors.
3. Appointments and reservations.
4. Quotations needing checking.
5. Shipments to trace and expedite.
6. Correspondence to be discussed.
7. Return requests.
8. Unusual catalog requests.
9. All new promotional materials (reminders to discuss).

In this successful model I made a supreme effort to keep it simple, based on my conviction that the others I had tried failed because they were too complicated.

Unless I had a folder on my desk to complete some action, I filed them by call sector so that they would be readily available for planning trips.

BENEFITS

A follow-up folder like this will greatly facilitate your ongoing planning. It will be your best reminder of the extra things you can do to accomplish the real purpose of follow-up calls, for example:

1. It will keep you aware of orders pending and the work that still needs to be done.
2. It will be an incentive to complete pending matters.
3. It will enable you to recall what was emphasized during your last call and to determine what further repetition is needed next time.
4. You will be able to review the status of all projects quickly.
5. Some system will be very helpful in planning each trip you take.
6. You will appreciate it most when your boss visits and you are able to bring him or her up to date on each prospect and customer. Your boss will appreciate that, too, and will be impressed.

SPECIAL FOLLOW-UP TECHNIQUES

There are a couple of very effective follow-up techniques for use between actual visits. One is the telephone. By its use, you can give fast answers to questions, and it provides a means of two-way conversations. Customers appreciate answers by phone.

Even if you have no urgent need to call a key account, it is a good idea to do that occasionally just to ask if there is anything you can do for him or her. The customer will be impressed with your thoughtfulness if you are on the other end of your territory. You might even get an order.

There is real support for the value of the telephone in the whole new marketing technique advertised almost daily on TV and in other media—telemarketing.

The other use is the use of letters. They serve multiple purposes. The first to come to mind is an immediate follow-up after an important call. That gives an opportunity to thank all involved in the discussion and to include some special emphasis of the major points covered.

If any questions were unanswered or any objections unresolved, a letter is a good way to handle them. You can research the answers when you get back to the office and express them in the best language by letter. You can also include any supporting data you have, with copies for all interested parties.

Letters are also excellent confirmations of phone calls and give you a record of the call and a summary of it.

Judging the value of letters is not simple. It is like appraising advertising. But on one occasion I got tangible evidence of their value, or at least of one letter. A manufacturer from Lima, Ohio, sent its personnel director to Dallas to interview for a sales agent for the Southwest. I applied and met with him. During the interview he indicated that he would return to Lima on the following Friday and would have a decision by the next Wednesday.

The timing allowed me an opportunity to write a letter. I told him that I appreciated the chance to discuss the company's need and to emphasize that I felt I could obtain the results his company expected. On the following Wednesday, I got the nod. Six months later he told me that the letter was the difference between the runner-up and me and the reason I got the job.

Since that time I have written many follow-up letters. There have been numerous expressions of thanks for them, but the most rewarding indication that they have helped has come on subsequent visits when the recipient has pulled out a letter I had written to him. He had used it and thanked me.

Remember This

A salesperson who conscientiously employs a good follow-up system is more effective than he or she can readily judge.

The system will help the salesperson maintain a smooth, steady effort, keeping the sales work moving forward.

It will contribute to gaining some of the professionalism of the most professional of all—the doctor.

FOLLOW-UP AFTER THE SALE

There is another specific follow-up that deserves your special attention—the follow-up after the sale. Attention to a purchaser after the sale can be used to your advantage in several ways:

1. It provides you with an opportunity to make sure that the customer is satisfied, and it is your responsibility to do so. If he or she is satisfied, be sure that this customer is aware that you have done your job well.

If all is not OK, do all you can to correct the problem.

A satisfied customer is your best prospect for additional business and much easier to find than a brand new one that must be developed from scratch.

2. Use the success to become even better acquainted with all of the customer's personnel. See the plant as frequently as possible. That can help you with similar manufacturers.

3. Frequently a satisfied customer will suggest other prospects.

4. In many cases, you will be able to obtain photos, references, application stories, and all of the ammunition you need for future presentations.

Keep your satisfied customers up to date on your new developments. Do not wait until they require something else. Create a new need.

Design your own follow-up system. Keep it simple and use it. Do not be plagued with the memory, as I am, of the many calls I made before I had a workable system, when I remembered something I failed to mention to a customer as I walked out the front door.

BE A PRO

For the professional, nothing less than a complete job is acceptable.

That completion is not left to chance; it is part of his planned effort in a systematic follow-up of all unfinished matters.

TERRITORY
MANAGEMENT
AND
DEVELOPMENT

chapter eight

Trade classifications

The structure of the industrial market can best be described on the basis of the trade classifications that have become so widespread.

GENERAL

The industrial market is vast. A lot of buyers are involved, and they vary greatly in their functions, methods, and policies. A lot of salespeople are both directly and indirectly concerned with this market and they need to understand its organization and operation.

Through the years, these classifications have been established and they give this complex market a sense of order. They have facilitated the categorization of these diverse purchasers and resellers on a logical and consistent basis.

One of the principal benefits from the broad acceptance of the trade classifications is related to pricing. To a considerable extent the classifications facilitate compliance with the myriad price and trade restrictions imposed by governmental agencies. Those regulations are intricate and complex, and their interpretation and explanation should be left to the legal professionals. For the salesperson, existence of those regulations should explain why some of the pricing policies laid down by their superiors often appear to be very stringent and why they should comply with them meticulously.

Related further to price, any fair-minded manufacturer or supplier (and most of them are fair-minded) want the prices they charge to be equitable, competitive, and able to return to them a reasonable profit for their efforts.

The most equitable criteria for a pricing policy consider what the supplier must do for the buyer (as in the case of the consumer) and what services that buyer (such as a reseller or distributor) can perform for the supplier. The trade classifications take all of that into account and facilitate the writing of a pricing policy.

Naturally, whatever the classifications are, the manufacturer (or other supplier) must sell its goods at a profit (at least for its total mix). The trade classifications help the company figure out how to do that and what segment of the market it can serve best.

The acceptance of the trade classifications has yielded other benefits, too. For example, the many trade associations that have grown up in recent years use these classifications as their guide for membership eligibility and for defining their goals to contribute most to the general marketing function.

THE CLASSIFICATIONS

To simplify understanding of the various trade classifications, think of them as a tiered structure like a totem pole with a high and a low end.

Those at the low end are exemplified by the industrial consumer. This purchaser buys for his or her own use and demands services from the supplier rather than performing any functions for the supplier. At the other extreme are the resellers, who buy to resell and, in the course of doing that, perform many functions for their suppliers. At the very top is the manufacturer's agent, who performs a complete sales function for a supplier though this agent does not buy for resale.

Because of the logic and universal need for such a classification system, some of the trade associations encouraged the use of colors to denote discount schedules for the various trade classes. At one time, the colors were used by most manufacturers and suppliers in the industrial field. Distributor discount schedules were blue, resale were yellow, industrial consumer were white, and the original equipment manufacturer (OEM) were pink.

Maybe that was the reason that a lot of aptitude tests I took years ago included a check for color blindness. Imagine the difficulty a color-blind salesperson could have using such multicolored discount schedules.

The principal classifications that have developed are:

Industrial Consumer
Reseller
Distributor
Original Equipment Manufacturer (OEM)
Private Brand Buyer
Manufacturers' Agent

To make the description of all of the classifications as consistent and thorough as possible, these points will be discussed wherever they are applicable:

Customers resold	Service and repair
Inventory function	Installation
Delivery service	Sales organization
Credit and billing	Advertising activity
Engineering assistance	Sales promotion

Industrial Consumer

An industrial consumer is any individual, company, or entity that buys a product or service for its own use or consumption in the operation of its business or service.

The range extends from the back-alley machine shop with one owner/operator who buys a few drill bits or hack saw blades to the largest manufacturing company in the country. Regardless of size, the industrial consumer buys for maintenance, manufacturing, or processing and performs no sales or service for the suppliers. The industrial consumer merely uses what is purchased.

Reseller

Above the consumer level is the broad area of manufacturers and distributors; the lowest of these is the reseller. The reseller is not established to qualify for a franchise directly from the supply source and/or does not supply the necessary services.

About the only buyer the reseller can handle is the industrial consumer, offering primarily services rather than products. The reseller is frequently a specialist, such as a metal fabricator, pump repair shop, air conditioning installer and repairer, millwright, or erector.

The reseller stocks some products related to the services performed, extends some credit, and issues invoices. The reseller delivers, offers engineering assistance, services and repairs, and usually installs new equipment. Some maintain a sales force but the smaller ones normally combine sales with other duties. The reseller advertises on a limited basis if at all and hands out promotional pieces furnished by the suppliers.

The price to the reseller is higher than the price to the distributor but does provide a margin for a reasonable profit on sales to the industrial consumers—especially if the parts sold are modified or complemented in any way.

The reseller is a vanishing breed and for some products, the manufacturers are not making any serious effort to save this role from extinction. Some suppliers have even eliminated the resale discount schedule. This development has come about because of the streamlining and consolidation of the distribution function to cut out unnecessary handling and expense.

Distributor

In a sense, the distributor is a reseller too, but his or her functions and activities are more diverse and the scope of these operations is much bigger. Distributors sell in broader geographic areas and often have multibranch organizations, much to the consternation of some of their suppliers who already have franchised outlets in the areas into which they spread.

Distributors qualify for a low price, which permits them to sell to other trade classes. To earn their position, distributors maintain substantial inventories and delivery vehicles to provide adequate service to the biggest plants in their areas.

Distributors often conduct surveys of customers' needs so that they can stock for almost any emergency, even for special parts in some cases.

Distributors offer complete credit and invoicing service and some carry slow-paying accounts, to their own detriment. That problem is compounded as the slow payers buy more and more from those who give the credit.

Some distributors maintain a repair station or modification facilities. Most provide a high degree of engineering capability for application of the products sold. Some even install equipment or provide installation through subcontractors.

The distributor has an adequate sales force, advertises aggressively, and participates in the cooperative promotional efforts conducted by his or her suppliers. Distributors are highly involved in their sales promotion and take part in trade shows, industrial fairs, open houses, training seminars for their customers, and all manner of other activities to spur sales in a highly competitive marketplace.

There is more about the distributor in Chapter Nine.

Original Equipment Manufacturer (OEM)

One of the big buyers for some products is the original equipment manufacturer (OEM). That is a company that buys a product for use as an integral part of the equipment it makes on a repeat basis for sale to its customers.

The description is intended to be restrictive enough to exclude any large company with capability to manufacture a special machine for its own use. To completely qualify, an OEM must offer its output for sale. A special unit for in-plant use does not qualify a builder as an OEM.

The OEM is a big customer for parts or materials for the machines that it makes, day after day, for sale. There are innumerable examples: manufacturers of pumps, compressors, machine tools, lawn mowers, air conditioners, appliances of all sorts, road building equipment, off-the-road machinery, special processing machines of all types, printing equipment, bottling machines, food processors, mining and oil field equipment, and myriad other machines.

Most OEM accounts build their own distributor organizations and maintain local branches to serve them and their local customers. They have their own sales organizations, and some of the branches function as repair centers.

The OEM spends large amounts of money on advertising, using all of the media—radio, TV, national periodicals, trade journals, and so on.

It must not be overlooked that the OEM does all of this only for what it manufactures and the parts it makes. The OEM does not distribute generally for several manufacturers in the same manner that an industrial distributor does. Even so, the OEM sells a lot of replacement parts for the supplier who furnishes the components for the machines the OEM builds.

All of this activity and the resultant volume of total purchases qualify the OEM for the lowest prices, except for the private label account to follow. Understandably, the competition for OEM business is intense.

In addition to the volume of purchases, OEM requirements make cost economies possible for the suppliers. Large-quantity orders for identical parts make larger runs possible to reduce set-up time. Parts may be bulk-packed to dispense with expensive individual packaging. Paper work is reduced considerably, as may be easily imagined when it is noted that an invoice requires the same costly processing whether it bills one hundred dollars or one hundred thousand dollars. Favorable production scheduling and a host of other money-saving shortcuts are possible in a large order for an OEM.

Some manufacturers and suppliers permit their distributors to sell to OEM's. The authorization normally applies to the smaller ones whose needs fluctuate and involve rather small quantities and more varied parts. The distributor qualifies to sell to OEM's by stocking parts and locally providing other services more economically than the manufacturer can.

In some instances, large distributors are authorized to sell even the large OEM's, usually because the local distributor is highly enough regarded by the customer that the distributor can swing the OEM's business. The distributor might also be able to do a better job than the manufacturer located in some remote city.

When the price structure is such that a distributor cannot compete for such large OEM business, the manufacturer who authorizes the distributor to sell to specified accounts grants a rebate or a commission to compensate for the services performed.

Private Brand Account

The private brand, or private label, account is an important classification, too. The distinguishing characteristic is that these companies buy a product made by someone else to sell with their own output, through the same outlets established for their own production.

The product may be made to special specifications or it might be off the regular production line of the supplier. In either event, the product normally bears the name, trademark, logo, or any other identification of the selling company rather than the one that actually manufactures it. Hence, private label or private brand are both common names for this classification.

Several factors have led to the growth of this classification and make its continuation beneficial for both the supplier and the purchaser. In some cases, the buyer is completing a product line to make his or her franchise more lucrative for present and prospective distributors. But the buyer does not want to spend the time or the money to design and tool up for the new product. Or, although the product is important to have, sales potential might not justify the investment needed to add it to the line.

In still other cases, the product purchased is such an indispensable complement to the buyer's own product that the two have to be marketed together. Yet the manufacture of the components is so vastly different that two separate industries are involved. The V-belt drive is a classic example.

The V-belt is a rubber product and is made by the rubber companies; the V-sheave, which along with the belt completes the drive, is manufactured by various metal machining companies. The manufacture of the two parts is so different that no manufacturer makes both parts or owns companies that do.

The rubber companies buy the sheaves on a private label basis and the sheave manufacturers buy belts on the same basis. Both of them aggressively market the complete drive, which is an important and widely used means of transmitting power.

For the supplier as well as the purchaser, a certain amount of private brand business is profitable and desirable even if the selling prices must be lower than through regular channels. Private label customers do not require some of the expensive items that are so important to the principal outlets for a manufacturer. Private label customers design and supply their own catalogs and price literature, and there are other economies in shipping, billing, collecting, and so on.

Private label accounts are customarily house accounts and no sales commissions are required. No special warehousing is needed, and usually private label customers are denied access to the supplier's regular branch inventories.

This is high-volume business and can reduce costs even on the production for sale through the regular channels established by the manufacturer. But the really important benefit is that it affords additional outlets for a manufacturer.

Pricing to private brand buyers is a completely different ball game. Obviously, they have to qualify for prices low enough to make their own manufacture of the product unattractive to them, and they must have the margin necessary to sell all of the trade classifications. They must be able to compete with their suppliers and to do everything their suppliers do except actually manufacture the product—catalog it, package it, engineer it, warehouse it, advertise it, and pay a sales force for selling it.

Manufacturer's Agent

There is one other operative in the industrial market that is not really a class of trade but that should be included to complete all of the marketing outlets. That is the manufacturer's agent. In the simplest terms, an agent is merely a salesperson for the companies he represents but is not a direct employee on their payrolls. The agent is an independent operator and is paid a commission for only the sales made or those made to the customers in the area assigned. In some cases, the agent warehouses for some suppliers for an additional fee.

Smaller companies that cannot afford the expense of a sales organization often engage agents. Even the larger companies sell through agents in those districts where sales are not adequate to support a direct, full-time salesperson. Agents can afford to sell on such a basis because they are able to represent several suppliers and spread their expenses among them all.

Remember This

Most salespersons must sell all trade classifications for maximum sales results.

Contemplate the various functions of each to determine their interests and their needs. Then tailor your efforts to satisfy all of their requirements.

Multiple Classifications

There is one other important consideration. Almost any purchaser can be categorized in two different classifications at the same time for different products.

Large industrial consumers buy lots of maintenance supplies, but they might also buy other products to sell along with their own production. These purchases could be on a private label basis.

Distributors are often resellers for some lines that they need to complete a service but for which they are not active enough to gain a distributor franchise. In such cases, the local distributor for that product sells them on a resale basis.

Among the OEM accounts this dual classification is most conspicuous. For example, consider a manufacturer of a line of industrial pumps. For all of the components that actually go into the pumps, this manufacturer is a legitimate OEM. But in operating a large manufacturing plant, that company would buy lots of industrial products for maintenance of the manufacturing processes.

As a matter of fact, some of the items bought and consumed in the plant are identical to those that become integral parts of the pump. All types of bearings are examples. For the bearings for in-plant use, the buyer is an industrial consumer. For those that go into the pumps, that buyer is an OEM. Bearings are expensive and they are expendable so, as you can imagine, price is an important consideration. As you might also expect, a purchaser cannot be too meticulous about designating the end use for bearings on every purchase order. He really is not concerned so long as the lower OEM price applies.

This same pump manufacturer could also be a private brand customer. Assume that there was a void in the line of pumps. The manufacturer might not be able to offer the distributor a certain size or type, yet the distributor might need such a model to better serve their mutual customers. It would make more sense to procure that missing model on a private label basis than to send prospects to a competitive distributor.

The benefit of the trade classifications from the standpoint of pricing should be emphasized. They simplify the writing of a fair and consistent pricing policy for the suppliers. They help, to a great degree, to ensure that all buyers, regardless of their size, receive fair treatment.

chapter nine

Distributors: selecting, signing, developing

The value of a distributor to a salesperson lies in the multiplication of the salesperson's effort.

It can be readily established that the distributor is the dominant factor in getting many products from the manufacturer to the ultimate user. A portion of the membership of just one trade association can substantiate that. A group of the members of the American Supply and Manufacturers' Association, Inc. sold nearly $4 billion worth of industrial supplies and equipment in 1980.[1]

ASMMA attracts general supply distributors. They classify the activity of their members into twelve product categories, ranging from chemicals for in-plant use to hand tools, to power transmission products, to rubber goods, to fork lifts, to cranes, and several others.

For nearly every one of the ASMMA categories, there are other trade associations of specialty distributors. None of those figures and none for those who do not belong to an association were included in the nearly $4

[1] Figure courtesy of American Supply and Machinery Manufacturers' Association, Inc.

billion. But even without them, the ASMMA total is ample proof to show that distributors have earned for themselves an important position in the overall marketing function.

TYPES OF DISTRIBUTORS

Distributors come in all shapes and sizes, but there are two principal categories: the general supply house and the specialty distributor.

The General Supply House

The classic example of the general supply house is the supplier that was once called a "mill supply" house. That label is still used by some who unconsciously reach back once in a while for a bit of nostalgia. This old type distributor might carry everything from nuts and nails to hack saw blades, to grinding wheels, sump pumps, engine lathes, belt conveyers, hydraulic power packages, wiping rags, king-sized brooms, and more.

It is tantalizing to some to find a really old-time mill supply house and to tour the vintage multistoried structure—to step out of an antiquated elevator, really little more than an ascending and descending cage, onto each planked floor in the building, observing huge coils of wire rope on one floor; seeing hose, rakes, wheelbarrows on another; and going on then to still another floor to find a complete gasket cutting operation in one corner and a belting shop where leather belting is still being spliced in another area. "Ah, what a reminder of the good old days," the visitor must say.

The modern counterpart still carries the assortment of industrial needs that are still in use, but its quarters are quite different This supply house still tries to service its clientele with just about all the day-to-day needs for keeping a plant running. Its big activity involves expendable, maintenance-type products.

Specialty Distributor

There is no better specimen of a specialty distributor than a bearing specialist, just a youngster, as compared with the old mill supply house.

This distributor stocks all types and most brands of bearings—ball bearings, roller bearings, needle bearings, full-size and microprecision, naked (unmounted) or mounted in pillow blocks and flange units, friction-type sleeves, and every bearing type or size you can imagine. The bearing specialist is literally bearing headquarters and aspires to be just that, as witnessed by the name adopted by one large distributor, "Bearing Head-quarters."

There are other specialty-type distributors, based on the products with which they are most involved—automotive, electrical, service station supply, rubber hoses, building supply specialists, barber and beauty shop suppliers, and others.

Aside from the different number and type of lines carried, both general supply and specialty distributors operate in much the same way, performing the specific functions that were listed in detail in Chapter Eight.

DISTRIBUTOR-MANUFACTURER TEAM

Manufacturers are very supportive of distributors and they should be. The supplier-distributor association is a team effort and has evolved for one basic reason only. It has proved to be the least expensive, most efficient means of moving product from maker to user, and there is more than one case history to prove that.

Several years ago a major manufacturer decided to sell most of its output direct to the large industrial consumers and practically abandoned its distributor organization. During that time, the company expanded to more than 130 salespersons and twenty-six branches across the country. With great reluctance, it soon had to admit that this was not the way to sell the product at a profit.

Now there are only a fraction of the salespersons and three or four depot warehouses. There are also some new executives at the top echelons. The primary efforts of the reduced sales force are directed toward estab-lishing and developing distributors, and they have regained much of the ground lost during the period when they circumvented the distributors.

As long as distributors earn their positions, as they do now, they will be a significant factor in marketing, and it looks as if they will be for a long time.

The chances are that your company has a well-defined policy applying to all aspects of distributor association. If so, you no doubt already have a distributor oganization. Whether or not it is complete in every important trade center, it is inevitable that some day you will have to find a new distributor. Some failures will have to be anticipated and require replacement; additions to your product line will demand additional outlets; or sheer growth in a particular area will make it impossible for you to maintain your market share with your present distributors.

When that time comes, you will have to select new prospects, sign the best one you can, and work with that distributor to make it effective. The establishment or expansion of a distributor organization will be discussed in relation to three major steps:

Selecting
Franchising
Developing

SELECTING

Before you even start listing prospects, have some form for accumulating and recording data about all those you contact. There is a suggested form in Figure 9-1. It may be easily modified to suit your needs, or if you have an aversion to such forms, devise your own system for recording all pertinent details.

You will need a complete dossier on every viable prospect before you can choose the one best-suited to your company. You will also find that the information you gather will help you to maintain a continuous awareness of the state of the district. It will help you answer questions and complete reports your inquisitive boss requires. It will also help you become the professional you want to be.

Preliminary Investigation

YELLOW PAGES. One of the best sources of prospects is the Yellow Pages in the local telephone directory. You will know that your

DISTRIBUTOR PROSPECT SURVEY   Date_____

                                               Telephone_____
_____
Name of Company

_____
Address

Personnel: Name   Title

               _____   _____

               _____   _____

               _____   _____

               _____   _____

Facilities: Appraisal of location and store_____

_____

_____

               Condition of inventory_____ _

Business data: Account Classification_____

               Manufacturers represented_____

_____

_____

               Area covered_____

               Number of salespersons_____ Rating_____

               Industries served_____

               Sales volume_____ Estimated Potential_____

               Credit Rating (D & B)_____ References_____

_____

Other comments and general appraisal:_____

_____

Figure 9-1.

competitor has used it when you check the copy in your motel room and find that several pages have already been torn out. The thief that has beat you to it has to be a competitor because who else would pilfer just the pages you want?

The Yellow Pages are an invaluable source of information. They will tell you very quickly a lot about your district even before you leave your room. They will show you who the distributors are and what lines they carry. They will also tell you which are your most formidable competitors and which distributors they have.

It always interested me as I traveled with salespersons that some of them always reached for the Yellow Pages as soon as they checked into the room. Others seemed to be unaware, or uninterested, that they were even there. But the memorable thing is that those who did not bother with them were the ones who could have profited most from a little more information about their districts, regardless of the source.

Be sure to check every classification that relates in any way to your industry. Run through the index first, and mark those you want to screen. Then go to those sections and list the names of all prospects.

Note the ads, but do not try to form any opinions from them. If you do that, you might find, as many of us have, that they can be very misleading. Those with the biggest, showiest displays are sometimes the weakest of all. They apparently feel that the most conspicuous ads impress their prospects.

Be skeptical, too, of those who show all of the major suppliers for any of the lines they have. The chances are that they do not have all of those lines on a direct basis. If they do, they probably will not do a very good job on one more.

It is unwise to eliminate or qualify any of the prospects shown at this time. I have literally drooled over a listing with an elaborate display only to learn later that my enthusiasm was unmerited. And there have been some listed that I initially thought would not deserve further attention but later found them to be excellent prospects.

OTHER DIRECTORIES. There are many directories other than the Yellow Pages. Those published by the trade associations are among the best; they list all of the members of those associations, as well as other information. At least one directory shows the suppliers of each distributor by means of a number code. Your own company will have copies for the associations to which it belongs. If not, a distributor will tell you which associations are important and how to get directories.

CHAMBER OF COMMERCE. The local Chamber of Commerce will be able and anxious to help you. Do a selling job on the local manager. Let the manager know that you have a valuable franchise for someone in the area, and he or she will gladly help you.

LOCAL CUSTOMERS. Another excellent technique for your preliminary investigation is to visit a few of the manufacturing plants in the area that use your products. Ask their purchasing people about who the best local distributors are. If you approach them right, they will give you a rundown on every one in town.

While you are calling on these local plants, get in a few licks for your products. If you create enough desire, someone might recommend your line to a local supplier.

GENERAL. By nature, the salesperson should be inquisitive, always eager to meet and talk with new people, and always willing to talk about his or her product with all who show interest.

Late one night a fellow worker and I learned about a big order in the lobby of the Lord Baltimore Hotel in Baltimore. (That dates that trip.) We were coming back from a ball game, and met in the lobby four men who were returning from what would now be called an extended happy hour. One of them thought he knew my friend. His mistake started a conversation and that led to a nightcap.

During the visit we learned that they were employees of a blue chip company and were in town to finalize a major plant expansion. Six months later my friend got a big order as a result of that casual meeting.

In all of my travels covering ten to twelve branches in the major cities of United States, I have spent a lot of time on commercial airplanes. Since most business people leave and return during about the same periods each week, it never surprised me that I might sit next to someone who knew people in my industry. On many occasions these visits, primarily to pass time, have provided information about a plant expansion, or new distributors, or something else to suggest prospects.

Think sales all of the time. Talk to the person next to you on the plane, or the person on the next bar stool, or even the barber in a strange town—if he gives you a chance to say anything. Keep your eyes and ears open and you might be surprised to learn how much you hear that is relevant to your interests.

Remember This

Your responsibility is not only to get the order. You also need to be continually finding new prospects, or your sales will dry up.

Use every means you can imagine to ferret them out. The more prospects you have working at all times, the more potential orders you have.

Your opportunity to multiply your efforts and to make your biggest gains is even greater if those prospects are distributors.

Casing the Area

The work of casing a town and investigating all prospects is often called "bird dogging." It is a tedious and tiresome job for most salespersons, and immediate results are a little vague. It is also time-consuming, but it is a vital part of establishing distributors, and the better job you do, the better distributor organization you can build.

Even if your preliminary investigation is not as productive as you had hoped or expected, there comes a time when there is little else to do but make some calls. Before you set out for that first one, plan your route to save as much time and motion as possible. Get a city map and circle the location of all of your intended calls. Then decide the best sequence and number them in order to actually detail your route through the city. I can tell you from experience that it is hazardous trying to plan your trip from a map while you are driving down a busy street.

MAKE APPOINTMENTS. With a detailed plan you can forecast your schedule closely enough to make some appointments. Do that at least for those who appear to be your best prospects. When you arrange an appointment, you immediately enhance the importance of the matter you want to discuss. You also ensure that you will be contacting the correct person who will be receptive to your call rather than being miffed at your interruption.

If you do not have the name of the person you need to see, exchange pleasantries with the switchboard operator. The best way to encourage help is to show some interest in him or her. Whenever there is any doubt, start at the top. You will get more attention from a subordinate coming down from the top than you will from that top person you finally reach after working your way up through all of the chairs. More than that, you need to reach the decision maker with as little lost time as possible.

Sometimes it is helpful to make a call even if you cannot make an appointment. Drop in and talk to the receptionist or visit the city sales desk and talk to the counter personnel. A lot of times you can learn a great deal from those people.

Do not lose sight of your chief purpose during these preliminary calls. Arouse interest to make your listener responsive. You also need to make your line attractive enough to create some desire if this distributor is your final choice. Plan your opening to attract the prospect's interest and then have questions ready to sustain the conversation until you learn what you need to know about the prospect. That is your reason to be there to facilitate your final judgment.

Take ample notes. Without them, your recollection of ten or twelve interviews will meld together into confusion. Your taking notes will impress upon the prospect that you are serious about the job at hand.

VITAL INFORMATION. There are several subjects about which you must have information before you can reach an intelligent decision about your best prospect:

1. Credit and financial stability—This is important and should be examined as early as possible to avoid wasting time on someone who could not pay the bills if you did make a sale.

Ask your credit department for help on this one before you start your calls and as soon as you consider one a prospect. Request that they obtain a full report. You cannot be effective if operating capital will always be a problem. In the case of some new distributors, you might have to shade these requirements or plan to help them financially on occasion. If this is a possibility, have a plan in mind and the authorization to offer it. Then do so only if other qualifications make it advisable.

For example, new organizations have special problems, but often a new firm, staffed with excellent people who are lean and hungry, is really the best choice. Many of the biggest distributors were able to start only because of such special help at the beginning. I once had a competitor who made a practice of helping new people get started. He wound up with the best distributor organization in the area.

2. Acceptability—Something else to decide early is the acceptability of the prospect. What will the prospect contribute to the image of your company? Is he or she ethical? Does this company have integrity? Naturally, the more respected your distributor, the better your chances for results. But the converse is equally important. If you take one just because he or she is available, it can cause you lasting damage.

You can tell a lot about this from observing the operation, its facilities, personnel, and general conduct of business. If you have serious doubts, double-check with the local customers.

3. Availability—In many trade centers there are supplier-distributor associations that cannot be pried apart. The distributor owner belonged to the same collegiate fraternity or sorority as did the president of his or her biggest supplier—maybe they are in-laws. If that is the case, forget it.

To be acceptable, a prospect must be available on the terms you have to offer. There is little chance with anyone else.

4. Organization—This is most important, especially the sales portion of it, both inside sales and the field sales organization. They need to be capable, aggressive, and successful, and they need to be people with whom you can work effectively.

Related to this is the general type of the distributorship. Is it a full-line house or a specialty distributor? If the former, does it have a special department for your product line?

Your choice of type depends a lot on the nature of your product. Here there are two broad categories—the specialty item or the commodity. An item is considered specialized when application know-how or a degree of creative sales ability is required to sell the product. A commodity is a simple requirement that can be easily ordered or sold by anyone who knows a part number or can otherwise designate what it is.

If yours is a specialty item, you will probably do better with a specialty distributor or a general supplier that has a strong department in your line.

5. Capability—Finally, it boils down to capability. What you want is the one who can do the best job for you. All other considerations are unimportant if this need is not satisfied.

There is a reason, too, that it needs mention. There was a time (and such periods seem to go in cycles) when there were a lot of old, highly respected, financially strong supply houses in many cities. They had been in the same family for many years but unfortunately the third or fourth generations were no longer ambitious. They had become dead on their feet.

Maybe that was the way some of the old mill supply houses suffered their final demise if they were not grabbed up by new blood. At any rate, there may be some of them still left, or something similar might recur. Avoid taking on a moribund distributor just because your credit manager thinks it is great or because you think you can bring the distributor back to life. That is too hard a job even for you.

Pay considerable attention to future growth possibilities and take the one that has positive prospects. Analyze what they have been doing recently and ask about their future plans.

6. Volume—One important index of a distributor's health is the volume of sales on your product. This is one of the most difficult answers for unskilled salespeople to obtain. They think of the question as being too personal or too confidential for them to be entitled to the information. This figure helps to establish quotas, set goals, and formulate sales programs.

Final Selection

When you have investigated as thoroughly as possible, you must make a final choice. You need the two best prospects so that you will not be totally defeated if the first choice does not accept your offer. It might require some juggling to keep them both working until you have made your final agreement, but keep both interested as long as you can do so without compromising good ethics.

To arrive at your choice for the two finalists, review the vital information described earlier in this chapter under "Casing the Area" and score each prospect on each of those points.

Remember This

Though casing an area is tiresome, you need to do the very best job you can.

Distributor franchises are long-range agreements and selecting the distributor deserves your most careful investigation.

A wrong choice can do damage that will be difficult to overcome.

SIGNING

Introduction

Once you have made your choice for your prospective distributor, you should expect to conduct a major selling campaign. Changing lines or adding new ones is serious business for a distributor. Neither of those decisions is made as easily as a buyer decides on a routine purchase. Signing a new distributor is more like obtaining the big order for an unusual capital expenditure. It takes time, and several calls are normally required.

It is especially difficult to franchise a new distributor in an area in which you have not been represented before. That places on your prospect the responsibility of introducing your line in the area. It might be even more difficult if you have lost a distributor for any reason for which you might be at fault. That might involve some image repair.

The Emphases

Signing, or selling, a distributor requires much of the same selling techniques and expertise that are effective in any sales effort, but as your good judgment should tell you, there are important differences in emphasis.

An industrial consumer buys the product for his or her own use and has interest limited to what the product can do. On the other hand, a distributor's chief concern is the profitable resalability of the products. The distributor and its salespersons must be convinced that your product will be totally acceptable and that it will offer increased potential for both sales and profit. The salesperson must convince the prospects that they can sell the salesperson's product and then train them, prepare them, and help them do that.

There are several areas in which the considerations of the distributor are unique:

1. Product—the product must be good, but primarily in the eyes of others. If the users of the product find the quality acceptable, the distributor can generate enough confidence to sell it.

2. Company—the more good things the potential customers know about the company, the easier the job of the distributor. The so-called famous brands are easy to sell. Presale advertising and promotion have

paved the way for the local salesperson. The mention of the brand eliminates a big block of the sales requirements.

3. Policy—different aspects of the supplier's policy are vital to the distributor, such as products included in the franchise (some products are best handled directly by the manufacturer because of their highly special nature); inventory requirements; stock adjustments and return privileges; terms and conditions of sale; advertising and sales support; and, most importantly, warranty.

4. Catalogs, price data, brochures, and so on—the distributor needs a full complement of sales literature which in itself lends support to sales efforts and simplifies the job. The users will settle for what will show them how to operate and maintain the equipment.

5. Training—distributors are more training-minded than ever before. The highly competitive industrial market has mandated that salespersons know their products thoroughly. This is especially true for the more technical items handled by the specialty distributors.

Consequently, training tools have become an important part of the merchandising package a supplier must offer to distributors. Most manufacturers have many excellent training aids: kits for sessions at the distributor's place, correspondence courses, factory school, packaged programs for conducting seminars for key customer personnel in their locality, and all manner of technical bulletins and product data sheets.

6. Promotional items—there are all sorts of handouts considered to be helpful in promoting sales and creating good will—cups, lighters, pens, golf balls, caps, and enough more to make this a field in its own right, the specialty advertising field.

The real value of these items might be suspect, but the need to furnish them is not. With one employer, we were laggard in getting on this bandwagon, and we had innumerable requests to join the parade of competitors who made them available.

7. Advertising—the value of advertising to the advertiser is beyond question. The dollars spent on it attest to that.

To the extent that it does facilitate sales, it is also a vital concern of the distributor. The distributor who is considering a new line wants to know about the prospective supplier's advertising program. The distributor wants to know what media are used and wants to see sample exposures. For the distributor, advertising is a feature of the line as much as the product qualities themselves.

8. Sales help—there is still another vital support program for many distributors—sales help or missionary help, actually making calls with the distributor's salespeople.

Most distributors expect such help from suppliers, and this is especially true if a new product or a new supplier is being introduced to the area.

I have done a lot of this because it was considered a major responsibility by one of my former employers. The executive vice-president of that company expressed his favor of missionary help. As regards stock replenishment orders for distributors, he said, "You cannot pour more into the top of the barrel until you draw some out of the bottom."

This subject relates closely to the development of distributors and must be included in the next section.

9. Competition—you will face competition when you try to add a new distributor. It has always seemed to me that there are never enough good distributors to go around.

But there is a more subtle type of competition that is easily overlooked. In a way, every supplier a distributor has is a competitor of yours, even if the products involved are not closely related. Those other suppliers are competing with you for the effort of the distributor's salespersons.

Very few salespersons do a good job on all of the products of their total line. They emphasize the products in which they have knowledge and confidence, those that they like to sell, and those that return them the most money. This whole subject must be given attention in both the selling and developing of a distributor.

The Sales Campaign

STRATEGY. All of the subjects discussed in preceding chapters and the experience and expertise you have been able to develop will influence your sales strategy, but you need to consider the two major peculiarities involved in selling and signing distributors.

The people are different and they have different interests. Instead of department heads, production people, plant engineers, maintenance personnel, financial analysts, and some of the others discussed as buyers, you will be more closely involved with salespersons and branch management in the multibranch operations. Few distributors will take a new line unless all of those people are completely sold on that line.

The other facet that must be given different treatment involves the buying motives and the unique emphases of those mentioned in the section immediately preceding.

PRELIMINARY SALES CALLS.   In preparation for your calls to sign a distributor, assemble the different selling tools you will need: product samples, policy statements, catalogs, price lists, brochures, training materials that can be displayed or shown and discussed, promotional items or a list of what is available, an advertising schedule with sample ad reprints, a copy of a distributor contract, suggested stocks to be inventoried, and whatever else you have available to make your sales calls more effective.

As early as possible, determine who will actually be involved in the final decision. Again, expect that they will be among others, the sales department and the branch management. Even if some of these do not appear to be directly involved, consider that they might be asked about their preferences.

While you are working on a distributor prospect, you should contact each part of the organization every four to six weeks, more frequently if you can schedule important discussions with the influential people. If it is a multibranch organization, this means that the total calls on the organization will be much more frequent, and they should be. This is an intensive sales campaign and it should be carried out and finalized as quickly as possible. When you have a good distributor prospect, sign the prospect as rapidly as you can. The distributor's interest might die or a competitor might beat you to it.

For your calls, adapt the suggestions in the previous chapters, especially those in the "Special Sales Considerations" of the "Anatomy of an Order," Chapter Three, and "Sales Presentations," Chapter Four.

Use each call to develop the information you will need for your final presentation. Try to anticipate the objections that might be raised.

Become acquainted with as many of the distributor personnel as possible. You will be surprised how much you can learn from a counter person, or a stock clerk, or even the delivery person. You will be given more freedom in a distributor's store, especially in the branches. Take advantage of that.

This development work will also provide you with excellent opportunities to study your competitors. If you are attempting to supplant a competitor, you must know all you can about that competitor's program, and this distributor or some of its employees can give you that information.

Use references in the same manner you would for any sales efforts, but in this case, some of the possibilities are more specific. They are among those who belong to the same trade associations as your distributor prospect. The directories will show you who they are and will list the names of the principals. Some of them will be your distributors, too, either in your territory or another one of your company's. They make excellent references.

Distributors are in the habit of visiting their major suppliers, so it is especially effective to invite key people to your plant. In many cases, they will insist on such a visit.

They are also more concerned about your management team, so it is important that they meet some of those individuals, even if they cannot visit your executive office. Take some of your executives to them. It is flattering for a distributor or a prospect to be visited by a high official of a supplier. The distributors like to show off their operations, too, and they feel important when someone from a supplier's top echelon visits them.

If the development calls have not led to a commitment more easily than you had expected, the time will come to make your final presentation. The most opportune time is when you have completed all of your planned sales efforts at all of the necessary locations and interest is at its highest.

There are a couple of other situations that might require you to make your move. If you have a competitor who seems to be gaining ground on you, make your ultimate effort.

If your campaign seems to be slowing and you cannot revive it, schedule your final presentation. You cannot afford to let it die on the vine.

Remember This

Convincing a distributor to take your franchise is much the same as any sales effort, but different appeals are important.

Analyze those appeals and plan, prepare, and execute your sales campaign to satisfy them.

Adapt in your effort every sales technique you know.

The Final Presentation

Your final presentation to a distributor prospect is similar to that detailed in Chapter Four. The only differences will relate to the points of emphasis and the materials you will need to support them. In regard to the latter, there is one special item you should prepare in advance. That is the list of stock components the distributor is required to maintain in inventory. It should be in such form that it may be used for the distributor's initial purchase order or, if he or she has a partial inventory of interchangeable parts, it should be usable as a check sheet for ordering the necessary fill-in stock.

You should also have a distributor contract fully prepared for signature.

Sometimes you can finalize the agreement one-on-one with the owner or manager in his or her office. Such an opportunity does not indicate that the prospect is less demanding or that your effort may be less conscientious. Have the materials you will need just as you would for a meeting with a large group. Be sure to have the contract fully prepared and a suggestion for the inventory.

In other cases, it will not be that easy and your closing effort is a full-dress presentation with several in attendance. Even that is much like the requirement outlined in detail in Chapter Four, with all of the props and preparations.

In selling a distributor in this final session, emphasize the complete program that you offer, including product, catalog and price materials, promotional items, training plans, advertising, sales help, and company support in general.

Cover all aspects of your policy in detail and ensure that it is understood. If it is a fair policy, it can be an important sales tool. In any event, it should be clarified early in your discussion.

Stress the aspect of the team effort in your association, and to highlight your contribution, have a schedule of your plans to get them off to a good start. Include these items:

Receipt of Initial Inventory
Receipt of Imprinted Sales Literature
Mailing of Distributor Appointment Notice

First Training Meeting
First Missionary Help Schedule
Schedule of Special Mailings

Discuss as your final elements the items that are cooperative, for which you both must agree on the scheduling. If this discussion and final establishment of the schedule is acceptable, you have already closed the sale. Just produce the contract and get it signed.

The Close

If the subtle effort just suggested did not succeed, then you will have to proceed to your planned closing effort. Be prepared to employ your favorite technique and have one or two alternates ready.

In some rare instances, a distributor will try to snooker you into permitting him or her to sell your line on a trial basis with no investment in stock. Avoid such an agreement firmly; it cannot work in most cases. Without a signed franchise and the necessary inventory, neither the manager nor the salespersons will exert much effort on your line. Your own support would be half-hearted and nonproductive. Many suppliers will not even sell to a distributor until the distributor has complied with all franchise requirements, and that certainly enhances the value of the supplier's line.

If you anticipate difficulty in getting a prompt commitment, there is one final technique that might be the clincher. Prior to your final meeting, make some calls in the area and sell something. Then have these orders with you at the closing session. At just the proper time, produce them as evidence that you have already started the team effort and have the new distributor's first order.

Or you might indicate that you already have some customers in the area whom you want to turn over to the new distributor for handling.

There is an excellent lead-in for the close of a deal with a distributor—the franchise that the distributor must sign. Bring that out at the psychologically favorable moment, go over it, and hand it to the distributor for signature.

Remember This

During the selling effort to franchise a new distributor, you will make many promises. Honor them.

If you are tempted to forget some of them, remember that you would have made even more if that had been necessary for the final close.

DEVELOPING

Once you have made the sale, you might like to think that you have done your job and are finished. Not so. It is time to go to work. The distributor bought your franchise because of all of the elements you told him were included and because of the promises you made.

In today's marketplace, top brands of any given product line are similar enough in quality that other factors become more important in their purchase and sale. Those other factors are the ones on which you based your well-prepared, well-delivered sales presentation. Your best guide to the work to follow should come from a review of those plus items in your line and the promises you made so enthusiastically.

Initial Stock

Your first obligation is to get your new distributor off to a good start. The first tangible indication that the distributor has a new line will be the receipt of the merchandise to display and to put on the warehouse shelves. Your chief obligation at this point is to ensure that the distributor's first order is shipped on schedule as completely as possible and that bright, new merchandise in good, clean packages is furnished.

Inventory Maintenance

Consider that the stock is more than just the material that the distributor must resell to make a profit. That inventory is a tool for efficiently servicing the customers in the local area. Through discussion and exchange of experience, you should have selected the sizes and models that sell in the area, and your quantities should have been realistic.

It cannot always work out that way, so you should have in your program some provision for a regular stock adjustment that will permit the distributor to exchange, at no great penalty, components that do not sell in the area for others that are more popular.

You really share with the distributor the responsibility to maintain the inventory as an effective sales tool. It will do neither of you any good if the distributor's inventory dollars are tied up in stock that will sit on the shelves while orders are lost because of lack of saleable parts. And this is not a one-shot responsibility for you. You should watch that inventory on an ongoing basis.

Most distributors expect their supplier representatives to take a stock check on each visit and fill in the holes. Some salespersons show a reluctance to do that, and that has always puzzled me. After all, the order is what it is all about. It is most confusing when a salesperson drives 300 miles on Monday to make sales all week with a distributor person and then does not leave enough time to reorder the goods sold. Until the computer makes all ordering automatic, ask for an order on every call and take time to wait for it to be signed. How else can your commissions accumulate? Or if job satisfaction is what you want, what can be more satisfying than an order?

Some distributors are prone to let their stock levels slip from the initial investment required to qualify for a franchise. My personal experience and comments of others confirm that distributors and their salespersons do the best on the lines for which their inventories are fully adequate. The salespeople can be most productive on products on which they can give instant service, and they are going to be urged by their superiors to sell what they have invested most in inventory.

There is another trap that a few distributors find difficult to avoid when they are located in the same city as one of your stocking branches. They become turnover conscious and like to work out of your stock. It is false economy for them and additional expense for you. It costs you more to handle the small orders, and it costs them inordinate expense for the extra pickups. Most distributors will cooperate to solve this problem if you show them that they are losing money.

Catalog and Price Data

Equally as important as the merchandise stock is the allocation of all of your catalog materials, price pages, brochures, bulletins, advertising and merchandising handouts, and everything that your company makes available on an ostensibly no-cost basis.

Such items should be ordered, imprinted where applicable, and shipped to arrive with the initial stock order or as soon thereafter as possible. An admonishment is in order here. Do not deluge a distributor with such materials just because the distributor is not billed for them. They cost your company plenty and indirectly they are an expense to the distributor. Money wasted on such items is denied from some other sales aid that might be more effective.

I have rummaged around a distributor's literature shelves and found huge quantities of price sheets and catalogs made obsolete three revisions back and, in doing so, have found the explanation for why our budget for that type material never seemed to stretch.

Maintaining the basic supply of those needs is almost as important as control of the distributor's product inventory. You can be sure that if a distributor has given you carte blanche authority over product stock levels, then the distributor expects you to give the same attention to other needs, such as your sales aids.

As you ensure that supplies are adequate, do one more thing—purge the stocks of obsolete materials as they become outdated. This applies especially to pricing data and brochures of products you can no longer supply. Destroy those to eliminate all chance for costly errors by innocent employees who will not readily forgive you.

Remember This

Ensuring that your distributor maintains an inventory of products to best serve its customers is as much your responsibility as it is the distributor's.

To have on hand the sales aids the distributor needs is equally important. Unless you equip the distributor to be effective, you will pay the cost in loss of sales.

Announcements and Other Mailings

A new distributor deserves an announcement from you advising the prospects in the area that this distributor is your authorized representative. Most companies have such an announcement form. If you have one, send that mailing at about the same time that the first order is shipped. If no form is available, write a brief letter and stuff the envelope with one of your mailers. The distributor should be able to furnish the mailing list and may even want to do the mailing.

Such a mailing is an inexpensive exposure, and there is always the possibility that your announcement will reach someone at the moment when there is a need for your product. An order could pay for the mailing and get your new associate off to a good start.

As your continuing effort in this respect, provide the distributor with other pieces and plan a mailing schedule. If you are skeptical about the benefit, consider how many companies sell all of their output of many different products entirely by mail. If the practice keeps them in business, it should benefit you.

Opening Sales Thrust

RECEIPT OF STOCK.   When the stock order is due to arrive at the distributor's place, or shortly thereafter, be there. You can be very helpful to many of the people in the organization. You will not have met some of them, but your acquaintance with them can be important from then on. Your being there will show your interest and your dependability; it will give you a chance to generate a little enthusiasm for the new line.

A simple explanation of nomenclature will be helpful to the stock clerks, and they will probably appreciate your suggestions about how to arrange the stock if it is a new line for them.

You can also assist in the setting up of the displays or models you have. Your being there will ensure for your products a prominent place in the display area.

At times when I have been tardy in attending to such things, I have come in later to find the initial shipment in a heap in the corner. There was evidence that it had been fumbled and moved and removed, but nothing had been done to put it into workable shape, and nothing had been sold.

KICK-OFF MEETING.   You want to make this initial effort a total barrage so that it will seem like a special event for the distributor to fire all the employees with enthusiasm.

This is the time to schedule your first meeting, an orientation or indoctrination session. This is an important meeting and will undoubtedly be attended by some who were not involved in the acceptance of your line. Some of them will wonder why a change was made or what new line they have to worry about now. This will be your chance to win their support.

If your product is completely new for this distributor, then obviously your subject matter will have to be more elementary. It might require two sessions on consecutive evenings. At least the following subjects should be covered in this first session to provide the minimum introduction to your line: nomenclature and part description, introduction to the basic catalogs, product application and selection, basic technical data, and pricing.

If you are supplanting a competitor, much of the basic product data will be familiar to your listeners. You will need to emphasize the differences in your product design and manufacture with stress on the advantages. Your objective will be to make them feel confident and comfortable selling a different brand.

You need to create your best impression for this first meeting. Put on a real show. You might want to hold it away from the place of business if facilities there are not adequate. You might also want to combine it with a dinner. Otherwise, all it amounts to is a few hours overtime for the rank-and-file worker, probably volunteered rather than financially compensated.

Most companies have complete kits for such meetings, or all types of sales aids and tools that may be used. The suggestions in Chapter Four, for a major sales presentation, will help you in your planning and preparation.

This is an excellent time to enlist the help of your product specialists and your sales superiors. Aside from their direct help to you in staging the meeting, their presence will show the extent to which your entire organization is supporting the cooperative effort.

End this one on a high note. It is a pep rally to some degree. You want to inspire and prepare all to go to work and sell your products. You want them to do a better job than they did before they had the line or when they carried that of a competitor. That is the only justification for their taking your franchise.

Based on special needs, you will want to schedule future meetings to advance the training of the employees or to keep their enthusiasm high. Establish a schedule for regular meetings with the manager after this initial success. Some are booked several months in advance.

MISSIONARY WORK. To make this a truly big week for your new distributor, combine some missionary work (actual sales calls) with the salespersons. The meetings will probably have to be held after hours so that all who need to can attend. This will leave the days free for some sales help.

The missionary work is a practical application of the training you are conducting. It makes a nice climax for the special promotion week. This will give you a first intimate look at some of the salespersons, and the overall impression you leave will determine whether your new partner is filled with enthusiasm or doubt about the decision to carry your line.

Missionary help involves a lot of hard work. It means getting out early and staying late, calling on the distributor's customers and making the most effective sales presentation you can. But it is a real opportunity for you. It can open doors that have been closed until now. On the first knock you get to the right person, and in many cases, no knock is necessary; the salesperson you are working with will walk right in. The salesperson knows the customers that well and takes you in as a friend, not as a stranger.

Do your best on these calls (as always). Show this local person that you know your products and how to sell them. Give the salesperson something to emulate after you leave. Make yourself wanted for future help. Even the distributor's other suppliers will be competing with you for his or her time.

While you are driving to your first call, ask for a briefing on what to expect. Discuss whom you will see by name, title, and job. Fix any names firmly in your mind and write them in your notebook. (Verify them later.)

Ask about the problems or prospects you might encounter and plan your strategy. Pinpoint the products that should interest the prospect most. Set objectives for the call, concentrating on elementary goals that will produce orders later if not today.

Between each call, critique the last one and make plans for the one to follow.

This is an excellent chance to continue the training of the person with whom you are working. Encourage this individual to ask questions. Cover any that come up as the result of a call. Emphasize the sales features of your line. You have the individual all alone in what is equivalent to a laboratory session. Take full advantage of that.

If you find that the salesperson has selected good prospects, commend him or her for that. Go out of your way to find something for which you can praise him or her. Do a selling job. If things have not gone too smoothly, give the salesperson some ideas on what might be planned for your next work together. Suggest other prospects and describe other applications in other areas which might be sold in this market.

Sometimes you will meet problems that you cannot solve on the spot. When this happens, take the details and send an answer as soon as you can. Until you become better acquainted with this distributor's prospects and customers, you are on trial with them. Do not let them down.

A follow-up letter for a good call can help you in more ways than one. It can be another step toward a sale and a reminder for the distributor's salesperson to follow the lead; and a copy of this letter for the manager of the distributor can show that person what you are doing.

Missionary help should become a regular habit for a salesperson who has a large distributor organization. He or she cannot afford to travel several miles merely to visit in the manager's office. Calls on customers and prospects should be scheduled for every trip, far enough in advance to allow proper planning. Distributor salespersons have lots of diverse lines, and they will do best on those for which they get the most help and encouragement. There is no better inspiration than an order, and if you help get it, you will be repaid.

Establish a list of the large key prospects in the area of each distributor salesperson. Make those accounts special targets. Call on them each time, and when one becomes a regular customer, move another onto the list. Carry ten or twelve on the list at all times.

Make a game of it. Add some excitement and competition among the distributor salespeople. Buy a steak dinner for each one who gains a new account. Salespersons thrive on competition, regardless of the value of the prize.

Remember This

Do your best to make your kick-off for a new distributor the most memorable the distributor has experienced.

Cover all requirements to ensure an auspicious start: arrangement of inventory in workable order, ready availability of sales aids and literature, training to equip the distributor to sell and order, and actual help in sales calls on key accounts.

Continuing Development

There are several other things you can do to solidify your position with your new distributor and to enhance the results of your team effort. You should do all you can to make this one of the best lines for this new distributor.

Stay alert to the price competition in the area. Compare notes with your distributors and try to keep them competitive with all reasonable pricing practices.

Ensure that your distributors are informed about all special promotions and help them to take full advantage of them.

Discuss your ideas for increasing business. Set an ambitious sales goal and then devise the plan to meet it. Keep all salespersons informed of progress and get them excited about it. Review purchase figures from your periodic reports with managers so that they know what they are doing at all times and how they are meeting the goals established.

Ensure that distributors make the most effective use of all advertising. Remember that this has been provided by experts at great expense. Do not permit a lack of knowledge about your company's advertising to detract from its value.

Do not try to impress any distributors by telling them they have a better deal than your other distributors. This will merely make them think that you tell that to all distributors, or they may think that you have more than one arrangement and wonder what your best one is.

Some distributors will try to gain special concessions from you. They may not even expect anything but simply deem the effort to get something to be always worthwhile. Scotch such requests fast and firmly.

When other distributors enter the conversation, do not be drawn out on volume figures or any other information that might be confidential. It will be only too evident to those with whom you discuss such matters that you have also revealed the same about their operation.

There is at least one other pitfall. For all of your fairness, support, and sympathy, be straightforward and aboveboard but do not mollycoddle a distributor or permit him or her to intimidate you. You have a responsibility to your company. Show the distributor from the start that it is a fair and honorable company and that nothing less than fair treatment is expected from the franchised distributors. Let the distributors know, gently but firmly, when they fail in their share of the effort. They will respect you for it.

BE A PRO

For salespersons who sell through distributors, the organizations they select and the manner in which they develop their organizations will have a profound effect on their success.

During the building process, the salesperson must be most diligent and must also practice the highest ethical and professional standards.

The final result will be a clear indication of how well the salesperson has done, because the best distributor organization of all suppliers stands out clearly. It also identifies the most professional salespersons and the highest caliber suppliers.

chapter ten

Planning
territory coverage

The individual assigned to a sales territory must manage that territory. If salespersons do not do that, the territories will surely manage them.

WORKING VS. MANAGING

There is a vast and readily discernible difference between just working a sales territory and managing one. I have known salespersons whose regular routine involved a trip to the office each morning (usually late enough to offend the office workers), where they shuffled a few papers, made a phone call or two, gathered a couple of items, and then took off. They had in mind only their first call. What happened after that depended on the results of the first call.

There have been others (though not as many) who rarely came into the office or, if they did, they were in and out before anyone else arrived. They knew where they were going that day and also on each of the next ten or twelve days. And we knew, too, through the reliability of the itinerary report they submitted in advance.

The latter managed their territories, and that was evidenced in a more indirect way; it was clear from the size of their commission checks.

MANAGEMENT REQUIRES PLANNING

A vitally important element of management is planning, and the essence of planning is the allocation of time. Your objective is to find the common denominator between the time you have available and the money you desire. Until you learn to develop a productive plan and to work it effectively, you do not really know what you are doing. To a large extent, you are just spinning your wheels, hoping that your frenetic activity will spin a few dollars of sales commissions your way.

I once knew a salesman who was made a territory manager on very short notice to fill a vacancy created by an early retirement. He was not really ready for the job, but times were good, it was a seller's market, and he did acceptably well. But about that time, a new sales manager joined us, who was gung-ho on selling smarter. He was very big on planning and stressed it because of the worsening of economic conditions that was being predicted.

My friend understood the new manager's message and, instead of being alarmed about less favorable conditions, he told me that he would double the production of the territory within three years. That introduction to the importance of planning was all he needed. He did double his volume in less than the three years, and he did it during a period when the market was very soft and while most of his fellow salespeople lost considerable ground. Within that three-year period, he was promoted to regional manager.

Some who do not fare as well often become totally frustrated and are ready to try something else. They decide that they might not have what it takes to succeed in selling and, while that is still their first career choice, they give up before giving it a chance. Help from a well-conceived plan might make the difference.

REASONS FOR PLANNING

There are several reasons why salespersons must plan their work if they are to be at all successful. Some of the obvious ones are:

They are required to plan their own schedules.
Their reports necessitate a plan of activity.
Planning saves time.
Evaluation of their performances is precise.
Planning can increase earnings.

Scheduling

Salespersons must schedule their own work and must plan those schedules themselves. They cannot just report to an office in the morning after breakfast on the run, check their IN baskets, and start moving papers; or they cannot sit and wait for the phone to ring; and they cannot check in with their bosses for another two-week project to put at the end of the present, frustrating four-week workload.

Each day salespersons must self-start, and they must do something based on *their* decision of what is best. Unfortunately, salespersons cannot even wait until that day to make their plans. That is what planning the coverage of their territories is all about, and without it, salespersons cannot manage their assignments.

Reporting

Much of the planning is mandatory because of the regular and special reports required from most salespersons. A weekly advance report of calls is an almost universal requirement for all companies. I know what it is to agonize over this report when its due date has arrived and there is no clear plan about what should be done during the week to be reported. I know, too, how much easier it is to complete the report when the plan of calls is well outlined for several weeks in advance and appointments are already scheduled.

Saving Time and Work

There are only so many hours a salesperson can spend in front of a customer. In a sense, the salesperson is paid by the hour—by those hours of actual selling, or trying to.

The very fact that salespersons' productive hours are limited makes it all the more vital that they waste not a minute of that time.

There is a lazy streak in all of us. It makes it difficult to find the time to develop a good plan. But a small investment in time once to devise that plan will save lots of time later.

Evaluation

Salespeople are in an unenviable position of being subject to precise evaluation. The performance of no other employees in the company can be as easily and objectively graded as that of salespersons. Their salaries, commissions, bonuses, and all expenses are tracked on a monthly basis, and at any time, their total cost to the company is known.

On the other side of the ledger, their production in sales and profits is equally clear and precise. Their individual contributions to the profit of the company are known by all who must check their value to the organization. Any comparison desired can be readily made—their present performance against what it was six months ago, a year ago, or whenever; and how they are doing as compared with a predecessor or any fellow salesperson. Planning for a more effective result could be the salesperson's best insurance for job security.

Earnings

The variable element in the compensation of most of those in sales is the important incentive. Their fellow employees in the home office and plant are paid a specific amount each month. About the only additional money available to them is occasional overtime, and even that is lost to salaried employees. Salespersons have no such limitations if part of their earnings include commissions or bonuses. The more effectively they use their time, the more sales and money they can make.

General

The value of planning first became clear when I was in a sales territory. But its benefit became even more conspicuous when I became involved in sales management. It was surprising how obvious it could be who managed their territories according to well-conceived plans and who just floundered around doing whatever the moment suggested.

It was always easy to predict who would meet a quota regardless of its size and what conditions prevailed. In a way it struck me that planning nullified the influence of bad breaks. The best planners made their own breaks and controlled them to be good.

THE PLANNING SCOPE

Almost all conscientious salespersons plan each call. They set goals for each, plan presentations in detail, anticipate problems and objections, and prepare accordingly.

After the call, they review the results, summarize all information important to follow-up calls, and consider any lessons that might help in future calls.

They also plan each day's work, even so far as to map their routes through the cities to save as much time as possible.

On a trip I took with one of our employees, we covered several cities For the first two, he merely pulled out a list of names and we called on those listed as we came to them. There was no problem in the first because it was small and there were only two calls. The second was much larger and new to the person with whom I was working. In the first day, we drove back and forth across the city several times. If we had planned our route first, we could have made several more calls.

Even more irritating was the fact that my companion considered himself excused because of his lack of knowledge of the city. Needless to say, we skipped the Happy Hour that evening and planned the next day's work in the room with a city map in front of us.

Remember This

You would not set out on a vacation without a plan. Most people would complete details down to the activities of each day to gain maximum use of the time available to them.

Your earnings undoubtedly determine what you can do on your vacation. Planning your work as meticulously as you would plan your free time will give you more money to spend during that leisure.

DEVELOPING
THE TERRITORY PLAN

Of all of the planning required for success in sales, none is more indispensable than the general plan for covering the territory assigned. A sales call that is unsatisfactory because of deficient planning wastes only a few hours at the most. It might even teach a lesson that can be used to offset the loss on that very day. But, when there is no plan for the overall sales coverage, most of the time is spent without a guiding purpose.

Fortunately, the subject of planning can be discussed to satisfy any planning need. The same principles apply whether the territory consists of two or three skyscrapers in Manhattan or two or three sparsely settled western states. Customers are pretty much the same, too, whether they ride a subway to work or commute thirty miles each way through light traffic from a home in a wide-open rural area. Products likewise do not distort planning principles.

Even more important, the benefit of a good plan to cover a sales territory is available in equal measure to the oldest, most experienced salesperson, or to the newest one to join the force. Whoever the salesperson might be, if his or her plan to use time is not the best possible then that individual is losing money.

Before discussing the actual procedure for developing a plan, it might be helpful to consider a preliminary overview of the major steps. Here they are:

1. Determine how the geography may best be covered.
2. Estimate the time available.
3. Translate that time into calls.
4. Establish a quota if one is not already assigned.
5. Calculate the number of dollars in sales each call must produce to attain that quota.
6. Assign to each prospect and customer a share of that quota.
7. Allocate the number of calls to each prospect and customer, based on the common denominator calculated in step 5.
8. Establish the actual cycle of calls.

A TYPICAL PLANNING REQUIREMENT

To make the planning procedure more realistic and more lucid, a typical requirement will here be correlated with the solution. This example has been chosen to involve all of the planning principles.

A plan will be devised to satisfy these conditions:

1. You have been assigned to a territory working out of the district office in the Dallas/Fort Worth metroplex.

2. The territory includes all of Oklahoma, all of New Mexico, and roughly the northern half of Texas. It is representative of the actual territories of many manufacturers and includes several industries, such as petroleum in all of its phases, agri-business, manufacturing of all kinds, high-technology industries, and processing operations of various types.

3. Your company is an old and respected leader in its field. There is a new sales and marketing team that has come up through the company. This team has initiated an expansion program.

4. Policy provides for both direct sales and for some products sales through distributors. The former includes systems that are engineered and sold by the company directly to the user. Replacement parts and maintenance items are normally sold through franchised distributors.

5. Customers include all of the trade classes described in Chapter Eight except private brand accounts and manufacturer's agents.

6. Sales and market figures are available.

7. Your quota is $1,800,000, an increase of 13.8 percent over last year.

Data and Tools Required

For the planning job you will need:

1. A list of all active customers with sales for at least three years, if possible.
2. A list of known prospects with potential.
3. A scratch pad and a columnar pad.

4. A felt-tipped marking pen.
5. A road map showing your territory on one side.
6. An adding machine or calculator.
7. An estimate of potential for each trade center.

Market potentials are very important, and your company should have those. If you have nothing, you must estimate them for planning purposes and then check and revise as you learn more about these figures.

There is an excellent source for market potentials for industrial products, The American Supply and Machinery Manufacturers' Association, Inc., 1230 Keith Bldg., Cleveland, Ohio, 44115. This association regularly publishes "A Market Research And Economic Trend Analysis of Sales through Industrial Distributors." Copies are available to nonmembers.

The analysis is based on actual sales reports by industrial distributors in twelve product categories. The total sales reported in 1980 reached nearly $4 billion[1], and that is a significant figure to project against the estimated total available. It will give you an excellent start on your estimate of the total market. The format is intelligible and manageable.

Almost any public library will have lots of sources for market data. Just a night or two a month in one of them while you are away from home should give you considerable knowledge of how big your market is and where it is located.

Preliminary Preparation

If you cannot find a map with all of your territory on one side, find all of those smaller maps necessary to piece such a map together.

Study the map with the purpose of deciding how you can cover the geography with a minimum of backtracking and deadheading.

Sector the map to divide it into routes or trips. Obviously you cannot work into the same trip points that are remote from the home base and that lie in different directions.

You should be living in the largest and most centrally located trade center, and that should facilitate your coverage. When you have decided how you can best cover the area, mark your map accordingly.

[1] Figure courtesy of American Supply and Machinery Manufacturers' Association, Inc.

It will help you to look at the map before you start and to follow these suggestions in marking it:

1. Draw a big X through your home base.

2. Circle all trade centers and any isolated localities where there is a known prospect or a customer. Designate with a "P" any area where you do not have a prospect but need one.

3. Outline sectors that could be efficiently covered in trips of one week. At this time, pay more attention to the physical coverage than to any volume or potential. Those will be considered later when you apportion your time. In some cases, a two-week trip will be needed to develop a sensible plan. Some salespersons still take two-week trips, but they fly back home for the weekend they might otherwise have to spend away from the family.

4. Bear in mind that not all of the area must be covered on every trip into that sector.

5. By the same token, it is unlikely that all sectors will be given the same amount of time or attention.

6. You should have six to eight sectors when you have finished.

7. Number the sectors.

Obviously, the establishment of the sectors is unique for each territory, and there is not necessarily only one way to determine them for any given assignment. In all cases, the objective is to provide for the most efficient coverage for the least backtracking and deadheading.

For the territory in our example, these are possible sectors that have been developed in actual practice:

Sector 1—Dallas/Fort Worth—to include the Dallas and Fort Worth trade centers of an approximately thirty-mile radius around each of those cities.

Sector 2—East Texas—the area east of the D/FW metroplex including Marshall, Texarkana, Longview, and Tyler.

Sector 3—Waco—the area south of the D/FW area, including Brownwood, Temple, and Waco.

Sector 4—Lubbock—the city of Lubbock and also Abilene, Midland, and Odessa.

Sector 5—Amarillo—Amarillo is the principal trade center in this sector, which also includes Pampa, Plainview, and Wichita Falls.

Sector 6—Oklahoma—This includes all of the state, with Oklahoma City and Tulsa as the principal centers.

Sector 7—El Paso/New Mexico—to include all of New Mexico and El Paso at the southern tip.

An additional example might be helpful and since Chicago is about the largest market hub that often includes rural areas, it is a logical choice.

Assume that you are assigned to a territory based in Chicago, including Michigan and Wisconsin and the northern halves of Indiana and Illinois. Potentially this is a larger area than one person can adequately cover, but many companies start with an assignment like this. For our purposes, it does illustrate the sectoring principles.

This area could be divided into these five sectors:

1. Chicago—the city itself, and Gary, Indiana.
2. Michigan—with the principal trade centers of Battle Creek, Bay City, Detroit, Flint, Grand Rapids, Kalamazoo, Lansing, and Saginaw.
3. Wisconsin—chiefly Green Bay, Madison, Marquette (Michigan), and Milwaukee.
4. Indiana—Fort Wayne, Hammond, and South Bend.
5. Illinois—Joliet, Peoria, Rockford, and the Quad Cities area.

In this general area, there are a great many prospects and customers for any given salesperson, in the rural areas and in the smaller towns and villages spread among the chief trade centers. They would vary considerably, based on the product or service sold. Some of these might dictate somewhat different sectoring along the lines of the principles suggested. Another important consideration for such an assignment is the greater density of industry, as compared with the Southwestern section of the country.

Determine Time Available

At this point you must determine as closely as possible what time will be available to you for working your territory. Decide first the number of days per year available for sales work. This time should exclude vacations, holidays, sales meetings, or even days you are going to be loafing around the office, much to the dismay of the sales manager. Here is a suggestion:

52 wks./yr. 5 days/wk. 260 gross working days
Less: Holidays   15
       Vacation   15 (3 wks.)
       Sales Mtgs., and so on   10
       Days in office   20
       Miscellaneous   20
Total days lost for calling   80
Net days for calling   180

Vary these numbers, as they apply to your circumstances, to provide the most accurate estimate you can of the days you will have for making sales calls.

The miscellaneous figure should take care of personal problems, sneaking out to play golf when your boss is out of town, muscle spasms the next day, spring fever, mad streaks, and so on. Just do not be too generous with this number, and if your conscience does not trouble you over it, be prepared for a surprise when you least expect it.

Now estimate the number of calls you can average each day, but first clarify your definition of a call.

Your company might have defined "call" for reporting purposes. If so, this will have no effect on that definition, but it will define "call" as used in this procedure.

Most calls are clear. You phone for an appointment or drop in unannounced (perish that thought); you are given an audience with one person; you present your story; and, it is hoped, you leave with an order. That is one call—not a very productive one if you just dropped in, perhaps, but a call. It is just *one*, no matter how long you waited to see your host or how long you spent with him or her after your patience had nearly run out waiting.

If one or two others were called in to hear your story and to contribute to the discussion, it would be fair to call that more than one call, to equal the number of persons involved, so long as that number was reasonable, not ten or twelve.

If you spend all day in a meeting with several persons, a fair count could be the number of those in attendance. Or if you want to be more conservative, you could allocate one day's worth of calls, based on your estimate per day.

Certainly if you visit various offices within the plant to talk to others, then each of them could be considered separate calls.

On frequent occasions you might make calls on customers with distributor salespersons. Count each business call with them as you do the ones you make alone.

If you work with a distributor in a trade show or if you conduct a meeting, use the number of calls you would normally make during that same time.

While telephone calls are very important and productive, they should not be counted, for the simple reason that our planning procedure and the allocation of time is based on personal visits.

This discussion is not intended to emphasize calls out of proportion. The subject is given full consideration to clarify the basis for the planning. Finally, you will have to decide. You can cheat only yourself, and the chances are that you will delude no one but yourself. Remember your boss has been out there, too. The boss knows all of the tricks and will recognize them more readily than you might suspect. That is one of the reasons he or she is now the boss.

Four calls per day is a reasonable goal, based on my experience. There will be days when you might make only one and days when you will travel all day in a rural territory. You should still be able to maintain an average of four effective calls per day if you are properly prepared and, even then, your expense per call will be unbelievable, as your boss has probably reminded you.

I know from experience that four calls are possible, even in an area involving considerably more travel than an occasional subway ride, very few of which are available in the great Southwest.

At four per day, these are the figures you will consider:

Calls per day	4
Per week	20
For the year	720

(36 wks., 180 days as est. before)

At this point, you need to know how many sales dollars you must generate on each call, to reach your quota. That is simple:

Quota	$1,800,000
Total calls per year	720
Dollars needed per call	$2,500

This does not mean that you must get an order for $2,500 on each call, though that would be great. It does mean that if you reach your quota of making 720 calls, that is what each must ultimately yield in dollars.

Allocate Calls

This is the meat of the planning.

At this point, the procedure can be described in most detail by the completion of a rather elaborate worksheet. Some readers might not need or desire such detail, so what follows is a summary of the principles of allocating your calls (and your time) in the most logical manner.

If you are curious about the more detailed treatment, or if any of the principles are not entirely clear, refer to Appendix B, page 179, where the longer, completed worksheet is given with a full explanation of all of the numbers.

This is the shorter procedure:

1. List all of your customers and prospects on the columnar pad you have (or one that you can easily line to provide four columns).

List them by sector with a page for each sector.

Show known prospects by name or, if unknown, show the trade center where you need them.

2. Study past sales and any potential figures you have for each account.

List any figures that will help you assign a quota to each one listed. Show at least that quota figure for each one.

The quota you assign represents the contribution of that account to your total quota. Include prospects, but base their quota on the expected closing date. In other words, you should not expect a total year's sale from a prospect who will be buying your products only half of the year.

Be sure that the individual quotas total your assigned figure, $1,800,000 in the example.

3. To determine the number of calls for the year a customer or prospect theoretically merits, divide the individual quota by the sales each call must produce. For the example, that was determined to be $2,500.

4. Allocate actual calls to each prospect and customer in each sector. The number determined in the previous step is a theoretical number of the calls, directly proportional to the contribution of each account to your quota.

In actual practice there are other considerations, and these numbers have to be massaged to be more realistic in terms of the special factors in each case.

Here are some examples of those other factors:

Generally, distributors demand more attention than other classes of accounts for training, sales help, and so on.

Some distributors require more help than others. They have more salespeople who require more help.

New distributors need more help until they are well qualified and able to sell your products.

Prospects for a large capital project need close attention until sold and satisfied.

Each active account deserves a minimum number of calls regardless of the theoretical indication.

The time necessary to complete all matters must be provided for each trip.

The number of persons you must see at each account must be considered.

Allocate generously to those customers who will give you the most volume at the least expense.

5. Total the calls for each sector. This will give you a clear picture of which sectors will be given the most time, and your overall plan should be taking definate shape.

Remember that all calls may be converted into time if that facilitates your planning. In our example, four calls is the same as one day.

Establish Call Cycle

Think of a cycle as the shortest period necessary to permit you to cover each sector at least once while you still hold to the ratio of total calls allotted to each sector.

The calculation to determine the cycle is fairly simple. Consider the sector that gets the least amount of calls. Assuming that you must give each sector at least a full week each time, list it for one week. Then assign time to the other sectors in the same ratio as the calls you allotted them in your final planning steps. For example, if your largest sector merits three times as many calls as the smallest, it will be given three weeks to each one week for the smallest. Simple division will give you the ratios among all of the numbers.

After allotting time in all sectors in that manner, add the weeks for all of them. That total is the number of weeks in each cycle. Each planning problem will yield a different result, but in the problem in the worksheet (page 191) the cycle turned out like this:

Sector	Weeks per Cycle
Dallas/Fort Worth	3
East Texas & Waco (combined)	1
Lubbock	1
Amarillo	1
Oklahoma	2
El Paso/New Mexico	1

What that really indicates is that each sector will be visited at least once every nine weeks and and each will be given the number of visits merited by its volume of sales. That works out to be four complete cycles a year (for thirty-six work weeks), and that sounds like a reasonable number.

PLANNING FOR URBAN TERRITORIES

Many sales territories are small enough that no overnight travel is required. This does not eliminate the need for planning. Time must still be allocated and call frequency determined. The planning principles already employed for the discussion of a rural area still apply. The task is merely less complex.

The biggest difference is that the sectors become sections of a great metropolis instead of counties and parts of states. Even in such an area, an orderly pattern of calling will save lots of time and travel expense.

Here are some suggestions:

1. Segregate accounts into sectors by general location.

2. Determine call allocation by procedure outlined.

3. Establish a call cycle, even if there are only four, such as North, East, South, and West, or if only two, such as Uptown and Downtown.

4. Cover the area by trips into the sectors as suggested, rather than back and forth across the city.

There is one other important factor. Travel time will be greatly reduced, and there will be much more time for customers and prospects, of which there will probably also be more. Save all of the time you can and use it just as frugally.

WORK YOUR PLAN

Assuming that you have done a thorough job on your planning, you should now feel confident that you know what your territory requires. To ensure that your extra effort pays off, you cannot afford to permit unimportant distractions from preventing you from carrying out your plan. Worse yet, you cannot let any developments induce you to scrap it in two or three weeks.

There are a few suggestions to help you guard against that and to keep your plan operative and effective:

1. Work according to the plan. Stick to it. Make minor revisions if warranted.

2. Plan around the nonwork weeks. If an unexpected one comes up, bridge your schedule over it.

3. If you lose a week unexpectedly, work it in at the first opportunity. In a really extreme situation, omit that week until the next cycle,

but use telephone contacts to advise your important customers and handle any problems that might result. Just do not permit one interruption to destroy your whole plan.

4. If you fall behind in several areas, block out a week (preferably at the end of a cycle) to catch up.

5. If nothing seems to work, do not panic. Analyze the problem and review your plan. With all of the details you have, that should be easy. Then make the necessary revisions, but be reluctant to give up your plan until you are sure that your execution is not causing the problem.

PLANNING TRIPS

When overall planning is complete, the next step involves the actual trips to make a complete cycle. Tentatively plan a cycle at a time. At least know the order in which you can best cover each sector.

Plan each trip in detail at least two weeks in advance. That much lead time is vital to enable you to make reservations and appointments or to confirm them. You owe it to your customers to give them some notice, especially in the case of a distributor, if you plan to work with some of their people.

The planning for each week is a progressive job. You have to be gathering well in advance ideas about what you will do each week and then bring those plans to completion as the week approaches. You must be considering more than just the next week or the one to follow that.

If you are beginning to think that all of your time will be devoted to planning, it is not true. Remember that you have allocated several days per year for miscellaneous needs other than selling. In our example, there were twenty for that, out of a total of 180 working days for the year. That is one day out of nine and you should be able to do a lot of planning in a little more than 11 percent of your time.

Much of your planning for trips will involve follow-up on various matters. To be most effective in that, some system of gathering and retrieving all notes on pending matters is a vital need. One possibility for such a system has been suggested in Chapter Seven, "Follow-up Calls." That can be a basis for your plan for each trip.

At least two weeks in advance, plan your itinerary in detail. A simple scratch pad was my best aid for this. I set up a page for each day of the week and listed the calls for that day. Beside each I made brief notes of whom to see and what to discuss. At the bottom of the page, I showed my hotel reservation. I kept this scratch pad on the seat beside me after the time I nearly ran off the road while trying to dig it out of my briefcase. That is where I had the supporting files.

There are a few specific suggestions that will help you plan productive trips:

1. Devise a plan that will enable you to complete all matters pending in the area.

2. Prepare specifically for each call before you leave the office to ensure that you have everything you will need for the call.

3. Gather all of the special files and other material you will need for the call.

4. You do not have to visit each account in each sector every time you go into that sector. Follow the guide of the calls you have allotted each one.

5. Plan your route to prevent deadheading as much as possible.

6. Plan some time for checking your competitive distributors.

7. Keep your customers informed of your plans and any changes necessary.

8. Be especially careful to take notes on all matters for follow-up to help you in making your plan for the next trip into the area.

Then, as thoroughly as you have planned every detail of your trip and as carefully as you have prepared to make it as productive as possible, go sell something.

BE A PRO

No professional would tackle any major job without first devising a plan.

To do that requires analysis of the task in all details and establishment of goals in order to measure progress and ultimate success.

Then the professional would execute the plan as well as possible, checking progress frequently to make any adjustments required.

And a true professional would expect or accept nothing less than total success.

part three

PROFESSIONALISM
IN SELLING

chapter eleven

Be a pro

*Regardless of the career a person chooses, every effort should be
made to attain professional status in that vocation. Judgement of
what has been accomplished is inevitable and the person who is
proclaimed a PRO by that final judge will be well rewarded for
his or her extra effort.*

MORE ABOUT GNP

There has never been more opportunity for a professional salesperson than
there is today. Consider again the GNP. In 1960, it was $560 billion—in
1980, $2,626 billion. In that twenty-year period, it increased fivefold. Of
course, economists say that those figures are not completely accurate, and
they are correct. The figures mislead because of price changes that took
place during the period. Those price changes distort the actual growth, because in the last ten years, prices have gone only up and that really means
that the value of the dollar has gone down. Today's dollar will not buy as
much as it used to, and since the GNP expresses the output of goods and
services in terms of the prevailing market prices, it is exaggerated.

The culprit is the old monster, inflation, and none can deny the hideous problems that it can cause. Inflation is an insidious affliction to any economic system. It can bankrupt and destroy a nation as devastatingly as loose living and profligacy can ruin an individual. It has done that throughout history, and even within recent memory in Germany, there was a time when a wheelbarrow full of marks would not buy a half-barrow full of bread at a day-old bakery sale.

A continuously declining price level can be equally damaging to an accurate evaluation of the GNP for any given year or period. In the years before 1972, declining prices prevailed, and that meant the dollar was really overvalued.

In order to make the GNP figures more realistic and more fairly comparable through a period of time, the economists have also expressed the GNP in terms of constant dollars. They have selected a base year, 1972, the last year before inflation started its wild trip of the last decade, and have adjusted each year's figures to compensate for price changes before and since that base year. For some years before 1972, that 1972 dollar would have bought more goods than the dollar prevailing in any of those years. Consequently, the GNP figures for those years were actually deflated, or less than they should have been. From 1973 on, the reverse proved to be the case. At no time since 1972 has the U. S. dollar bought what it would have during that year, and those inordinately high prices have artificially elevated the GNP.

Trusting the revised figures resulting from the constant dollar values, there has still been a terrific growth of the output by American citizens in the last twenty years. Consider the GNP in constant dollars, or again, in dollars in which the influence of price changes has been completely wrung out. Based on the value of the 1972 dollar, the GNP was $737 billion in 1960, and in 1980, it was still more than $1,480 billion. That is more than double the 1960 figure, and I submit to you that any nation that can double its productivity in a short twenty-year period can accomplish progress that is well beyond reasonable criticism.

OTHER SIGNS OF PROGRESS

But even that does not tell the whole story. No society in the history of mankind has enjoyed the level of affluence found in the United States today. All sorts of figures could be cited to support this dogma, but figures are dry and in many cases fail to really impress. In my thinking, nothing can be more graphic than a trip into the stores and food markets followed by a return home to tune into the evening news with scenes from Poland showing queues at a market in which the shelves are stripped bare before the waiting line can be even noticeably dented, or to hear later in that same telecast about the abject poverty that characterizes more than half the nations of the world.

There is even more spectacular evidence that things have changed since 1960. The products and services that have been introduced are unbelievable. In plastics, electronics, transportation, communication, medicine, and other fields, there has literally been an explosion of new and amazing discoveries and innovations.

Consider your own household. Think of the changes in the telephone—from a three- or four-party line with a big ugly box on the wall with a crank-operated bell to the sleek, decorous, new instruments on which direct dialing from one end of the country to the other is possible.

I have a special appreciation of this from a recollection of a personal experience. It goes back more than twenty years, but it is even more spectacular because of that. In the late thirties, I had occasion to call on the phone from central New York to Madison, Wisconsin. For a three-minute conversation on a barely acceptable connection that took at least five minutes to complete, the charge was $7.50, an amount that seemed massive and was, in terms of the prevailing value of the dollar. On my last telephone bill, there was a charge for a call from Dallas, Texas, to central New York for which the charge was 85 cents. I dialed the call myself in seconds and talked for a full three minutes with no need to repeat or ask for a repeat of a single word.

Walk through your home, and in the kitchen and utility room, note the appliances you now have—washer, dryer, garbage disposal, compactor. How different is your stove from what your parents used? How about your air conditioner and heater? Consider the house itself. Most people in this country have a better domicile than the one they deserted to seek their own success less than twenty years ago. And now when young people leave home, they drive away in their own cars. What kind of car did you have when you left home?

The progress in medicine is mind-boggling. The heart may be completely exposed to the open heart surgeon while its capability to perform the functions that sustain human life is being repaired. Amazing cures in other medical fields have eliminated what used to be inevitably lethal diseases.

Communication and transportation have been revolutionized to the point where the planet on which we live is no longer big enough to challenge us. Only the universe is now a large enough theater for our research. We have tackled outer space, and some of our contemporaries have walked on the moon. And we watched them, live on TV, by satellite.

Granted, all of these accomplishments have not been initiated and fully accomplished within the last twenty years, but there is hardly an area of our existence in which the state of the art has not been refined, expanded, or amplified in ways that we would not have dreamed possible in 1960, when the GNP was $506 billion in terms of the dollar of that day, or $737 billion of what the 1972 dollar would buy.

The fact of the matter is that additions, improvements, and totally new things have come so rapidly that we take them for granted. A mere two years after we have gained a specific innovation, we can no longer remember the days when we were without it. We expect progress and no longer have the patience to wait for it.

It all sounds almost too good to last. But it will last. It must, because as nearly unbelievable as our progress has been, it cannot slacken seriously for very long. The more a nation learns, the greater becomes its capacity for further learning. The greater the lore of basic information that can be assembled by a society, the faster will be its progress in further spectacular growth of the knowledge bases to spawn even more and more progress. The more problems for which an understanding can be reached, the more rapidly that understanding can be spread to completely expose new and baffling subjects. And in no respect are these truisms more applicable than in the area of material things, the things of which GNP figures are made, in any dollars.

THE IMPORTANCE OF SALES

But from the standpoint of GNP-related progress, there is an element that is equally as important as a large base of knowledge from which to work. It is the machinery to ensure that the products developed will be applied and sold. It is wishful thinking for the builder of a better mousetrap to believe that those plagued with that rodent will beat a path to his or her door. They will do no such thing; exterminators will outsell the mousetrap builder who sits back and waits. That is what makes the role of the professional salesperson more secure and more potentially rewarding than it has ever been. The role of the real pro in selling is vital to the future growth of the GNP, and this professional will be afforded opportunities for success that have never existed before.

With such a personal stake in the future, it behooves an ambitious salesperson to reach for that professional status as rapidly as possible. Success will come to no one automatically any more than it will to the sedentary inventor of the better mousetrap.

ESTABLISHING GOALS

Before salespeople can consider success from the standpoint of something they, themselves, will reach for, they must have some idea of what it is that they are seeking. Unfortunately, classical definitions help very little. The entire concept of success is such a subjective consideration that definitions mean little. We all become inarticulate when we try to describe what we mean by success, even though it is a personal matter. Worse yet, we can describe it for no one else, and no one else can help us in deciding what it is for us. It is not the same for all individuals. What might be totally rewarding success for one can be complete and frustrating failure for another.

It is that very subjective nature that makes it possible for individuals to set goals for themselves if they have the ambition to excel in any endeavor. But one thing is clear: if one is desirous of attaining what he or she deems is success, then he or she must set specific goals, study and plan a course, and expend the effort necessary to accomplish the purpose.

Patterns of the success of others can be profitably studied. The case history method for such a study can be helpful. All one has to do is to list what one thinks are the requisites for success; histories of individuals who have reached comparable goals are well documented for study. The individual can study those traits that contributed most to the success of the subjects and then set out to emulate them.

But historical characters are remote and not always easily understood. They might not make the best subjects. Even as much as has been written about famous, successful persons, most of them remain nebulous personalities, as compared with the acquaintances with whom we spend our everyday existence or with whom we are at least contemporary. And even though contemporaries might not have developed their success to the point of total confirmation, as a historical person might have, almost any individual of any age has some acquaintances who have established a reputation worthy of trying to match—a boss, coworker, minister, teacher, coach, or other locally respected citizen.

In thirty-five years of selling, I have met any number in all areas of the country; in all walks of life; of all ages, creeds, colors, political inclinations, or philosophical outlooks; male and female. In all of those who have established the greatest promise for success, there have been clearly discernible, strong points of character and conduct. These elements, common to all of them and important to their success, suggest the qualities that one should work hardest to develop as he or she defines goals for personal success and begins to work toward attainment of those goals.

QUALITIES OF THE SUCCESSFUL

Successful people are thinkers. All of the intelligence in the world is practically useless unless it is employed on a full-time basis. It is the thinking process that utilizes and exploits intelligence. By thinking, one can analyze, draw conclusions, and direct his or her actions. The most dismal lapse of thought is often characterized by a remorseful remark, "I just didn't think about that," or "I guess I just wasn't thinking." And the most dismal part of the last example is that if one has to "guess" that he or she was not thinking, then that one is still not thinking.

Thinking might not be any more important for salespersons than it is for any other professional, but it might contribute more to their success. Many of their experiences cannot be programmed in advance, and that leaves only the thinking process to signal the correct response to the various situations encountered.

I made a call with a salesman one time who was a graduate from a prestigious university. He obviously had the necessary intelligence, because his degree was in a demanding, technical field. During the call, we determined early that this was not really a prospect for us, but during our conversation, the interviewee suggested a good one in the same city. After the call, I asked my companion where we should go next. He checked the preplanned itinerary and observed that we were all through in that city and should go to the next on our schedule. I asked why we should not visit ABC Company (the prospect mentioned in our previous interview). His reply was, "Yeah, he did mention them, didn't he?" Did he have a mental lapse? Was he just absent-minded? Not really. He had heard as his reply indicated. He just had not thought.

For all salespersons there is one important element of thinking. It has to be more than just plain thinking. It has to be *positive* thinking. When a salesperson doubts that he or she can get the order, failure is inevitable. I have worked with salespersons who have told me before an important call, "We're going to get this order," and it has happened, sometimes when I questioned that likelihood. Was it a hunch on the part of the salesperson who called the shot in advance, or just a boast, or wishful thinking? In most cases, I really believe that it was nothing more than *positive* thinking.

Many of us fail to realize that positive thinking on our part can have an effect on those to whom it is exposed. Few would deny that when they are in a positive frame of thought, they can be more effective in accomplishing their purpose. Such thinking is closely allied to faith. Those who have faith that they can do, most often can do. That attitude has a material effect on their efforts. But I am convinced that there is another dimension to such positive thought. It is discernible to the person to whom the positive thinkers are speaking, and that person finds it more difficult to resist the speakers' efforts to convince him or her about whatever it is that they are speaking—in the case of salespersons, to deny them the order.

There are some who even say that the power of positive thinking extends a favorable influence over immaterial, external factors in our success. They believe that we can influence circumstances to prejudice our success. I cannot doubt that. There have been too many accomplishments by too many people who ostensibly had none of the tools for the unexpected achievement.

Thinkers are the best planners. They develop strategies for their efforts and they execute according to their plan. They are never too busy working to think about the requirements of their jobs. And no task is so small or so automatic that a plan for its completion is unnecessary.

Attitude is an important element of success. A good attitude requires a healthy outlook, a sense of feeling right about whatever one is doing. Time after time, NFL professional football players and other athletes, in interviews with the press and TV broadcasting teams, credit attitude for their outstanding performances. When asked why they think that they are doing so much better this year than last, they often say, "Well, I think my attitude is better this year."

Certainly the converse is true. Few athletes can produce when their attitudes are jaundiced by preoccupation with a contract dispute. During such periods it is their attitudes that suffer—much more visibly than their pocketbooks.

Ambition might be a facet of attitude, but however it is classified, it is vital for success. One who lacks the eagerness to excel has little chance to do so. It is difficult to recognize successful people who are not literally consumed with ambition. They are clearly driven by strong desires, impatient to be hard at the job at hand.

Attitude toward others is especially important for a salesperson. The salesperson must possess empathy. If one thinks that success is contingent on denying something from others, his or her entire thinking process is likely to be so distorted as to render him or her ineffective. Empathy toward others enables a person to think as others, and to do that is nowhere more important than in selling. It is vital to do that in order to know how the one to be sold is thinking.

In a solid attitude, there is a noticeable air of expectancy. One of our outstanding salespersons once became almost totally unproductive over a very short period. We talked to him and our conversations revealed some attitude changes and problems, but those did not fully explain his sudden loss of effectiveness. Late in one conversation, after nearly all imaginable approaches had been tried, I suggested to him that the most puzzling thing was his slide from the success he had generated just a short time before. His reply was, "I really didn't expect to do that well, and I doubt that I can continue like that." My response was, "Jack, we expect you to do that well, and a lot of your friends do, too. Certainly your expectations for yourself should be as high as those others have for you." Within three months he was back on the track and then he had an air of expectancy.

To a significant degree, a person's attitude affects his or her patience. Few have not heard the expression, "the patience of Job." If you have not heard it, read the book of Job in the Old Testament. Job kept his faith, patiently expecting that things would get better even when his world was falling apart around him. Even the best salesperson will lose more orders than he or she will get and, without a generous amount of patience, a few lost orders will turn into disaster. Failures test patience, but they also provide the very best learning experiences. On the other hand, a person in quest of success cannot afford to be too patient. Whenever patience passes over into complacency, chances for success are materially diminished.

A sense of direction is indispensable to success. As much as any other quality, a sense of direction is clearly a factor in success. As early as high school some have distinguished themselves as "most likely to succeed." Those who have earned that accolade and who have gone on to justify the faith of those who selected them for the title have not always been the smartest in the class. What is it then that has inspired the prediction well founded enough to be confirmed later? My recollection tells me that those I thought way back in high school would have the best chance for success were the ones who already knew where they were going and had at least the first stages of their routes already planned.

Most of us have goals, but we fail in their attainment for several reasons. The biggest cause for failure is that those goals are too amorphous. Their definition is so vague that we cannot decide upon the paths to take toward their accomplishment. If we just happen onto a right course, we cannot properly gauge our progress to the extent that we know that we should push on straight ahead or slightly modify our direction. Our effort is finally reduced to mere wishing or hoping.

Those I know who have succeeded have had clear goals. They have always known what they wanted to do and what accomplishments would constitute success for them. And these were not vague, unspoken goals—something to shoot for if the opportunity presented itself. They were clearly defined objectives, broken down into logical, orderly, well-delineated stages in an attainable sequence. They held no chance for failure because of being too remote or too foggy.

When I started interviewing for salespeople, one of my recollections of questions that had been asked of me in similar interviews and on personality inventory tests was, "What do you expect to be doing five years from now? Or ten?" I, in my turn, asked these same questions, and the education afforded by the answers was surprising. When an interviewee responded without hesitation just where he or she expected to be in five, ten, twelve, or any number of years, it was somehow very simple to envision that the person would be there on time or ahead of schedule. Conversely, when one answered with a shrug, "Oh, I really have not thought too much about that," his or her desirability as an employee immediately plummeted. In many cases I was later given an opportunity to judge the progress of some of those interviewed. Without exception, few reached any elevated positions they had not defined and worked into their plan long ago, and few who had done that failed to reach commendable levels of accomplishment.

The value of ambition and industry is greatly diminished unless it is directed on a well-planned course. Even the best-laid route is less helpful if there is no chance to check progress regularly. Homing instincts to keep us on the track are great, but they are neither scientific enough nor reliable enough for the entire trip.

The individual with a keen sense of direction and purpose is conspicuous. That becomes obvious when one hears again and again about a young person on the move, "He knows where he is going," or "She knows where she is going."

Success requires adaptability. One of the most successful persons I know is an eighty-year-old man. The surprising thing about him is not that he has come so far and accomplished so much. He was the embodiment of the determined businessman forty or fifty years ago, so his early success surprised few of his acquaintances. The truly amazing aspect to me was the fact that he finished just as he started—a man of his era whenever that was. He was just as contemporary in the modern world in which he finished as he was in the one in which he started. He adapted to changing times. He did not permit them to pass him by. He never felt sorry that the old days had gone nor yearned to have them back. From all appearances, one would think that he had never heard of the word "nostalgia." For him every step into modernity was a challenge to be met every day. He was not dragged ahead by change; he managed to stay ahead of it.

Things are constantly changing and, oddly, most people resent that. As a matter of fact, an easy guideline for recognizing the potentially successful is to note their reaction to change. The one who recognizes and welcomes a well-considered change that will likely be an improvement and gets with it with vigor will not be daunted.

Adaptability involves resiliency. Adversity is inevitable. The individual who can meet that development rather than resigning to it has the capability to succeed. That person accepts a bad break as a challenge rather than a setback, changes the plan to profit from it rather than lose, and then presses on with more diligence than before. He or she never questions whether it is worth the effort and does not back off.

Pride is a key ingredient in success. Pride comes in for a lot of bad press, and there is no doubt that false pride is a most despicable trait. But it is most objectionable only when it is misplaced or unwarranted, and the fact that it can be a mixed blessing does not detract from its desirable qualities.

The satisfaction of doing a job well should be a justifiable source of pride. But it should come before the accomplishment and then can furnish an inspiration for the one who is attempting a difficult task. One who sets out to do something who has no pride whatsoever in the result will most likely have little success from the endeavor.

Dependability and consistency characterize success. In recalling classic examples of successful people, those who come to mind early are the ones who have been most dependable and consistent. They could always be counted on for their best performances and they were always consistent enough to be adequate for whatever the requirements might be.

There are always some in an organization who are capable of an occasional, dazzling performance, and those results, even though rare, are never unappreciated. But they can be, and often are, followed by miserable failures. Even if the overall achievement averages out to be creditable and fully acceptable, something is less than commendable about such an erratic record.

The conduct of a successful person is exemplary. One indisputable sign that a person has attained a confirmed degree of success comes when others start to emulate that person. When someone is good enough to become a pattern for others who are also trying to succeed, the success of that person copied is acknowledged.

Exemplary conduct is closely related to leadership ability which, in its turn, is a most important requisite for success in some fields, including selling. An individual must be respected to be effective in a leadership role, and one's respect can be gained or lost by what one says and later supports with his or her conduct.

This is proved by the fact that a leader in one activity will almost always be among those who lead in other areas. The same exemplary conduct that gains respect among some will most likely do the same among others.

Few successful persons are short on enthusiasm. One of the most contagious traits of all is enthusiasm, and successful people who can profit from the enthusiasm of others can also most easily inspire others by their own enthusiasm. Few can be dull in the company of a lively, dynamic person who is displaying zeal and zest for what he or she is doing. The converse is also true. A dull demeanor that exhibits what is close to distaste for even being around will produce the same lethargic indifference in others.

This has been illustrated for me through several years of membership and participation in a particular church. The pastor always set the tone for the congregation, as would be expected. This was nowhere more noticeable than in the receptivity of the congregation for a sermon. When a stimulating address could be anticipated by an enthusiastic preacher, there was always a noticeable eagerness to become more alert to avoid missing a word. When a dull, listless discourse delivered in a half-hearted manner was all that could be expected, there was a shifting of the physical positions of all in the corporate body in the church. The men seemed to lay back to assume a posture of mental tranquility, but their wives became especially alert against the chance that they might need to nudge a spouse to keep him awake.

Even in the church school classes and other subordinate organizations there were doers and resters, based on the leadership of the group. This was particularly obvious as the leadership changed from year to year. When an enthusiastic team led a class, few members could stay away from the regular sessions and the special functions. But under unimaginative, unspirited leaders there was always a noticeable drop in participation and general interest.

Enthusiasm will get business for salespersons. I was making calls once with a fairly new member of our sales group, who had made a very good start with us. Naturally, he took me to visit a fine, new customer whom he had added. During a tour of the facilities, the manager and I had an opportunity for a few private words. He told me, "That man you have out here now is really a good one. He is so enthusiastic I just could not turn him down."

All who succeed are industrious. This is an indispensable require-ment. No one who is too lazy or unwilling for any other reason to devote complete attention to the mission at hand can hope to succeed. The only reason such a successful person watches a clock during working hours is to see how much time is left for the project underway. And even working hours for this individual are not the same as they are for others. There are no boundaries for the working day. When the office closes, this person will likely still be there and will, as he or she finally leaves, carry something along to work on later.

Not one of my acquaintances was a harder worker than a boss I once had. His day started earlier, ended later, and lasted longer than did that for anyone else in the company. And every night he took home a full brief-case. He worked on what he took home, too, according to a remark his wife once made to me. Even on the golf course, this person never forgot the job. On the few occasions when I rode with him and while I was thinking of my next shot, he would bring up an observation or question about some phase of our activities or plans for increasing business. And oddly, his golf game was still very creditable.

Success reduces to achievement. I have never met a successful person who was not a habitual achiever. You might say, "How could you expect otherwise? One who succeeds must obviously achieve." But I am not refer-ring here to the ultimate success that confirms achievement. The one who succeeds started early with successes and rarely broke a winning streak. When this individual did, the resultant failure was only a temporary set-back, and even then, it was a learning experience and an inspiration to do more and better.

The mental attitude of achievers is different, though its uniqueness is only subtly apparent. Sometimes they seem almost subdued or humble, and you rarely hear of their achievements from them. You hear about their accomplishments from others. But that impression of humility can be mistaken for the serenity that comes from the immensity of their faith in themselves. Achievers know what they have done and know how to follow their successes with even more. They do not need attention nor do they need to prove anything to themselves or to others. All they need is a chance to do what they know they can.

It takes faith to succeed. There is one final trait that most of the successful people I have known have had in full measure—faith. They have had faith in themselves, of course. That sort of faith has already been discussed in positive thinking, because it is the basis for such thinking. But they also have faith in others. They trust them and they depend upon them. It has struck me that only those who have faith in themselves can trust and depend on others. How can a person who thinks he or she can do nothing hope for any better performance from anyone else?

There is another kind of faith that shines through the makeup of the successful. They have, almost without exception, a faith in something bigger than themselves. But whatever it is, it is more than just an object of faith. It is a source of strength and an inspiration.

No one can make it entirely on his or her own, nor is anyone expected to do so. For the one who will accept that, it will be easiest to place faith in some higher power and in other people. It will probably also be easiest for this person to succeed.

THE WAY TO PROFESSIONALISM

If my appraisal of the talents and qualities requisite for success is accurate, they certainly apply to the attainment of professional status for a salesperson. They also provide the first assignment for the one who wants to study to reach that goal. Analyze the successful, design your own composite, and then do your best to emulate that composite.

For the effort beyond that, there are a few specific suggestions in addition to what has already been said, possibly repetitious, but relevant to success in sales and too important not to emphasize in these final words.

Study Selling

That might sound like odd advice, but there are a great number of books about selling on the bookstore shelves today—some good, some bad. A truly ambitious salesperson should have difficulty passing up what looks like a good book on selling. Even if it proves less than expected, it will be worth the effort to read it, if it yields just one idea for a sales presentation or a closing technique.

One title that every salesperson should possess and of which the pages should be frayed from use is the original classic, *How To Win*

Friends and Influence People by Dale Carnegie, the same Dale Carnegie who founded the perennially helpful course on self-improvement for any career. This is the primer for all sales study. It exposes the basic philosophy of selling.

If you cannot find any sales books, consider those related to the subject of rhetoric. That is where you can learn about persuasion, written and spoken, for a friendly or hostile audience.

Study the conduct and words of others and learn from them. A person who will assume that he or she can learn from any associate or acquaintance will rarely be disappointed. Learn from your boss when he or she travels with you. Accept the boss's visit as an opportunity instead of a bad break and disruptive element. Learn, too, from the distributor salespeople with whom you work. They are constantly on the firing line. Or, if you are a distributor salesperson, profit in the same manner from your work with those who represent your suppliers.

Cultivate Sales Instincts

I knew a fellow who had to become a professional salesperson; nothing else would satisfy him. He took an aptitude test for a sales position and failed it miserably. The counselor told him that he had none of the instincts of a successful salesperson and that his best career choice would be something entirely different. Two years later he tried the same thing for another company. When the counselor told him how well he had done, he reinforced his statement by saying that his test results had virtually matched the ideal personality profile for a salesperson.

In the two years intervening between the tests, he had read every sales book and article he could find. In some of those there were tests, and he administered them to himself. But he did not try to learn any pat answers because he had been told that such a technique would not work on the tests. His approach was different. He used all of the material he read and all of the tests he completed to expose and define the basic qualities a sales job demanded, and then he worked to cultivate those traits. Before he took that second test, he had convinced himself that he was exactly the extroverted, empathetic, self-motivated charger he needed to be to become a top salesman.

When he told me this, my first thought was that there was something fraudulent in such a method and that it surely would backfire for him.

Then, shortly after that, I read something by a testing authority to the effect that a person who would do such a thing could actually have great potential for success. The rationale for that seemingly illogical statement was that anyone who desired a sales career enough to study its demands with such diligence would have a head start on a successful career. Several years later the individual just described proved both himself and the testing authority correct.

Develop Empathy

Empathy is a quality that can be practiced, but it is one that many salespersons do not give the consideration it merits. Just one small dereliction involving that has always amazed me. Many salespersons seem to make little effort to get names straight. Missing a person's name is tantamount to insulting that person. We all know that, because we know how we feel when someone misspells or mispronounces our names. Make a habit of getting business cards on every call and keep them up front before you file them until the spelling, pronunciation, and precise title on them are fixed in your mind.

Think Positively

The advice on this is short and simple. Try it again and again. The first time it works for you will prove to your satisfaction its tremendous power, and it will give you some insight into how to employ this amazing technique regularly. For a very special dimension of the use and power of thinking positively, read *The Magic of Believing* by Claude M. Bristol, published by Prentice-Hall, Inc.

Work at Selling

Plan your work. Plan your overall strategy and plan each call and presentation. A good plan will help you accomplish the other requirements. A plan is the very cornerstone for positive thinking. The metaphysics of that is simple. A well-prepared plan inspires confidence, and that pushes out the negative waves that inhibit positive thinking.

After a failure, indeed after all calls, hold your own personal and private critique. Review what you did right and where you could have done better. That practice will nurture instincts that will soon automatically produce the right reactions in all circumstances.

Some people feel that they should reward themselves after a laudable accomplishment. Some salespersons, for example, feel entitled to the rest of the day off after they have made a good sale. Others push on even harder. They assume that events have turned in their favor, and they want to exploit that break as quickly and as fully as possible.

Act Like a Professional

Carry a briefcase on all calls. It was not advice that taught me that but a personal experience. Expecting a short, unfruitful call one day, I called on a purchasing agent with nothing except what I carried in my pockets. To my surprise, the purchasing agent asked me about a piece of our equipment. I told him that I had a very descriptive brochure in my catalog in the car and that I would go get it. He said, "No, don't bother this time. I'm pretty busy. Show me next time." A month later I came back, and since I had done one thing right—make a note of his interest—I immediately showed him the unit that had been mentioned. He said, "Oh, that. I had to move faster on that than I expected and bought it just the other day." He continued to look at the brochure and then made one final comment, "Gosh, I wish I had waited. Yours looks like a better unit."

> Carry a briefcase and use what you have in it.
> Make a sales pitch every time.
> And finally, ASK FOR AN ORDER EVERY TIME!

ULTIMATE SUCCESS

You might be asking yourself how all of this extra planning and work are going to pay off. Maybe, you are thinking that it could be a lot easier and equally profitable to lay back and just take it as it comes. Your first success should indicate the rewards that are possible—the personal gratification, the extra commission, the immediate enhancement of your reputation, and the praises from all of your coworkers. A big order will make you feel great all over.

There is another reason, too. It is easier to extend yourself than to half-try. That lesson came to me during my first days in the army during World War II. Languishing around casual pools during those early days, some of the men surprised me with the energy and connivance they used to avoid work of any kind. One man in our company was especially diligent about escaping all duty assignments. Then one day he showed up for a detail. He was there the next day, too, and he worked. I could not resist asking him why he had changed so much, and he told me, "It is easier to just work; feels better, too."

All of such thoughts will probably inspire you to question the very basic nature of success. What should one consider success, and how can one recognize it? Is there a minimum amount of wealth that must be accumulated? Is there a list of feats that must be accomplished? A degree of popularity to attain? A rival to surpass in some respect? Just what does it take?

My answer may be conveniently oversimplified, and it can apply for anyone. When one can truthfully say to oneself, "I have done the best I could with the opportunities and the resources I have had," that individual's success cannot be denied.

Appraisal of the success achieved will be easy for all, and that includes you. Some day, sooner than you think, you will face a review of what you have accomplished. And the judge will be much more demanding than you ever envisioned.

I can aver that because I have already faced one judgment. It was the inescapable one that follows a major career segment. It came for me when I retired from regular employment. And the judge I faced was really tough, just as yours will be some day.

That is funny, too, because I know the judge. I know him very well, and you will surely know yours. In my case, I was that judge, judging my own performance.

And now there is one last hope—I hope that when your day of judgment comes, the judge can rule with conviction that you BECAME A REAL PRO.

Binder for
sales presentations

When you have a meeting with a large group to present your final effort for an important sale, you want to make it something special. Use all of the sales tools, and prepare and plan to make your ultimate presentation as impressive as you can.

One thing that adds an extra embellishment to your offering is an assortment of supporting data in an attractive binder or proposal folder, personalized for each one who attends the meeting. Beyond its utility, this binder adds a really professional touch.

IMPROVISATION

Many companies have a binder for such use, designed and prepared by their advertising departments or agencies. The basic information is attractively printed, and there is a ready means to add the special details applying to the individual meeting needs.

If your company provides nothing like that, the challenge is to prepare a binder in a professional manner in small quantitites. Whatever you use must be thoroughly high class, or the positive impression will be negated. If that might happen, you would be better off to just pass out what your listeners need.

It is possible to make your own cover with the help of a well-qualified advertising and catalog clerk who has some imagination and paste-up skill. A basic three-ring binder or some other suitable vehicle can be found at any well-stocked office supply store. For a reasonable price you can have your message silk-screened on the front, or you might be able to buy a label in small quantities to stick on the cover.

FORMAT

Whatever you have affords an opportunity to set a theme for your meeting and to state that right up front. Your own imagination and knowledge of your special purpose for your meeting will guide you in stating its theme. As an example to show what is intended, something like this should suffice:

A PROFITABLE DISTRIBUTORSHIP FOR XYZ SUPPLY

or:

A COST SAVINGS SYSTEM FOR GADGETS GALORE, INC.

But you can do better than that. Your company name, logo, and so on, should be shown lower on the cover.

There is another feature that will enhance the appearance and help in another way. Personalize each binder with the name of the recipient in a bottom corner. That adds a nice personal note and can benefit you in the placement of the attendees to best suit your advantage. Always try to seat a suspected heckler between two of your best supporters, never next to each other if there are going to be two of them.

CONTENTS

Include in the binder only the items that you know will be discussed or relevant to your discussion. It should not be cluttered. If it develops that other material will be used, that may be passed out later.

Here are some of the items you will probably want to place in the binder:

1. A title page—this should contain a statement of the theme, a designation of the prospect for whom prepared, and again, the name of your company. It is nearly a repeat of the cover for emphasis.

2. Contents—you might want to include next a page to show the contents.

3. Attendees—list, in some attractive pattern, the names of all who will attend, with titles or job designations of both their people and yours.

4. Agenda—here show the subjects you will discuss in outline form, headings only. Do not hesitate to include the final items most pertinent to the closing of the sale—contract, purchase instrument, or something else on which a signature can signify the purchase. After all, you are there to finalize a sale and there is no need to be subtle about that.

5. Exhibits—include any brochures, tech bulletins, and other such items that will support or emphasize the advantages of your proposal.

6. Contract—include that purchase instrument, whatever it is, prepared for signature by the prospect.

7. Extra space—stick in a few sheets of paper for any notes anyone desires to make.

BENEFITS

The tangible benefits of this sales tool justify the extra effort to furnish it. Here are some of them:

1. It clearly defines your proposal and your plan to present it.
2. It carries the necessary supporting data in an orderly fashion.
3. It evidences the thought you have given to the planning and preparation of your proposal.
4. It makes an excellent working tool for you and your helpers.
5. It adds the professional touch that sets your company apart and increases the respect of your prospect.

I have used such a binder on several occasions and very rarely has it failed to inspire several compliments. On one occasion when we failed to make the sale to a distributor in Dallas, we got great grades for our effort. Though the grades added little commission for us, they were gratifying and they proved to me the soundness of the idea. The many sales that followed so easily and so naturally were the real proof, and that proof became clear in the commission checks.

Detailed worksheet
for allocation of calls

If you are new in your territory or if you need a more detailed analysis of it than suggested in the procedure outlined in Chapter Ten, a more elaborate worksheet should satisfy all of your requirements. An example is shown in Figure B-1.

On a columnar pad with twelve or thirteen columns, mark up a sheet like the sample on page 180. You will need one worksheet for each sector and one for the ALL SECTOR totals. There are slight differences in the requirements for the ALL SECTOR sheet, but the one form may be easily adapted to that.

If you are fortunate enough to have all of the figures, this will provide you with an analysis of where you stand, what is available to you, and how to allocate your time to increase your market share.

In those cases where you have to guess or estimate, do so with the intention of constantly checking your figures as you become more familiar with your territory. In the meantime, stick with your best estimate until you are pretty confident about how it must be changed.

After assembling all of your sales and potential data, complete the worksheet for the ALL SECTOR totals first. It will be easiest if you

Sector _____ Worksheet for Planning Territory Coverage _____ Year _____ Quota _____

1 No	2 Customer or Prospect	3 Location	4 Acct. Class	5 Estimated Potential	6 Sales Last Year	7 Percent Penetration	8 Quota Next Year	9 Inc. Over Last Year	10 Calls Theo	11 Sched	12 Weeks Theo	13 Sched
1												
2												
3												
4												
5												
6												
7												
8												
9												
10												
11												
12												
13												
14												
15												
16												
17												
18												
19												
20												
21												
22												
23												
24												
25												

FIGURE B-1. Worksheet for planning territory coverage—blank.

complete columns 1 through 9 on a line-by-line basis. In other words, complete the first nine columns on the first line, then go to the second line, and so on.

Here are the instructions for each column:

COLUMN 1—No.

Show the number you have assigned to the sector.

COLUMN 2—Customer or Prospect

This column is for the name of the customer or prospect. If the prospect is not known by name, show "Prospect" or some other means of identifying an objective.

On the worksheet for ALL SECTORS (which you will complete first), show a name to identify that sector as you will think of it or refer to it. Use the name of the principal city, or twin cities, or state, or section of the state. On this first sheet, you will show the totals for the sector in the other columns.

COLUMN 3—Location

Give the location of the customer or prospect. (Nothing necessary for the first sheet for the sector totals.)

COLUMN 4—Acct. Class.

This column is for a symbol to represent the type or classification of the account, as described in Chapter Two. Use your own designations or something like these:

Distributor	D
OEM	O
Consumer Sold Direct	C

Add a P after the above for a prospect

Having this information in front of you will help later, especially when you begin to apportion calls.

This column will not apply to the sheet for the sector totals.

COLUMN 5—Estimated Potential

Show the potential you have. Of course, that will be the total for the sector on this first sheet and for each customer and prospect on the other sheets. If you have no confirmed figures, estimate as closely as you can.

In this column on the sheets for the customers and prospects, the figures for each line will not add up to the total for the sector because there are accounts that you do not sell but that should be included in the total potential.

COLUMN 6—Sales Last Year

Show total sales for last year in column 6—totals for each sector only on the sheet you complete first. For the sheets for each sector, show the totals for all of the accounts and prospects listed in that sector.

COLUMN 7—Percent Penetration

It will be helpful for you to know what share of the total market you captured last year, and that is the purpose of this column. To obtain the figure, merely divide your sales last year by the estimated potential, and express the result as a percentage. In other words, it is column 6 divided by column 5. This figure will help you in breaking down your quota by specific account for the year, and in directing your efforts in the longer run. Moreover, if you intend to *manage* your district, you will recognize this as a figure you must know at all times.

COLUMN 8—Quota Next Year

Show quota for next year in this column. Columns 6 and 7 will help you set this figure, and this is the time to recall the figures for any previous years you might have. Study all that you have available and try to set a realistic figure of what you can produce next year. Consider the rate of increase and take into account any factors you know of that will influence your effort.

If the figures have been given to you, columns 6, 7, and 9 (when you have 9) will give you an idea about where your greatest difficulty should lie.

COLUMN 9—Inc. Over Last Year

In this column, show the percent increase over last year. Divide column 8 by column 6 and show the result as a percentage to get that figure. It should be over 100 in all cases where you expect an increase, and the amount over 100 is the percent increase.

Before going to the next column, complete all of the lines for the rest of the sectors on the ALL SECTOR sheet. Show at the bottom of the page all of the totals that are applicable. For column 8, that total must equal your quota, or you have more work to do.

Completed thus far, the ALL SECTOR sheet should look like that shown in Figure B-2.

The remaining columns should be completed for sector totals but not on a line basis. For the remainder, it is easier to complete each column entirely. Then if there is any massaging to be done, it will be less troublesome.

COLUMN 10—Calls-Theo.

This column is included to tell you the theoretical number of calls merited by each customer or prospect, solely on the basis of purchases, and your figure of what each call must generate. For ALL SECTORS, each line shows the total for that sector. This is really your benchmark that would apply if volume were the only consideration.

To determine the figure, divide column 8 (the assigned quota) by the figure you calculated necessary from each call to produce your quota. In our example, that was $2500, and that is the figure we have used in the specimen solution (column 8 divided by $2500).

Remember it will be best if you complete this column all the way down so that you may check to ensure that your total equals the number of calls you have scheduled for the entire year.

COLUMN 11—Calls-Sched.

In actual practice it will not be in your best interests to apportion your calls indiscriminately on such a theoretical basis. All of your customers and prospects will not require the same time or attention that is proportional to their purchases.

Worksheet for Planning Territory Coverage — Year 1982

Sector All sectors Quota $1,800,000

COLUMN	1 No.	2 Sector	3 Location	4 Acct. Class.	5 Estimated Potential	6 Sales Last Year	7 Per cent Penetration	8 Quota Next Year	9 Inc. over Last Year	10 Calls Theo. Xched	11 Weeks Theo. Sched	12	13
	1	Dallas/Fort Worth			4,000,000	600,000	15.0%	710,000	18.3%				
	2	East Texas			750,000	110,000	14.7%	120,000	9.1%				
	3	Waco			150,000	36,000	24.0%	40,000	11.1%				
	4	Lubbock			1,500,000	200,000	13.3%	230,000	15.0%				
	5	Amarillo			800,000	145,000	18.1%	170,000	17.2%				
	6	Oklahoma			1,800,000	340,000	18.9%	370,000	8.8%				
	7	El Paso/New Mexico			1,200,000	150,000	12.5%	160,000	6.7%				
		Totals			10,200,000	1,581,000	15.5%	1,800,000	13.9%				

FIGURE B-2. Worksheet for planning territory coverage—complete through column 9.

Column 11 is provided for your adjusted figure, which will show you the number of calls considered optimum for each account, based on its particular needs but guided by the theoretical numbers.

Column 11 is one of the most important. It really amounts to the apportionment of all of your time for the year. Yet you are going to take those numbers you have so precisely developed and arbitrarily change them all. That might cause you to wonder why everything should have been so exact until this point.

Really it is not inconsistent. To be less exact at the start would provide no data worthy to be the basis for judgment at this stage. It is like the building of a machine in a way. In order that parts may be put together in random sequence or in order that they might be used to replace any worn-out part in any machine, they have to be cut to demanding tolerance.

If tolerances were inordinately loose, several parts could deviate in the same direction so that the aggregate variance would make a fit impossible. Normally one part will vary one way and another the other way so that the deviations from perfect offset each other, but that is never ensured. For example, if the tolerance is too loose and every part is cut on the high side, or tight side, the parts would not go together.

But if a given part is always the last to go into the assembly, it must simply fit well enough to be installed and perform its function. So it is with our plan. After this point, it is possible to introduce flexibility that is desirable.

Here are some further explanations for the figures in column 11:

FOR AMARILLO-80 Calls

I did not start with the Dallas/Fort Worth sector. On the premise that rural areas have to be allocated a minimum of calls to make a full week's trip, Amarillo and El Paso/New Mexico seem most logical to consider first.

The calculations specify sixty-eight for Amarillo, but that would not provide even weeks of work for this remote area. Nor would any less than eighty calls permit at least four trips of a week each for the year. Eighty, therefore, seems to be a minimum, but there is no good reason for making it any more than that. Because of its limited potential, the four trips a year should be adequate to hold our present position in that sector. If any problems or unusual opportunities arise, time can be diverted from another area for special missions out there.

EL PASO/NEW MEXICO—80 Calls

Here again eighty calls appear to be the minimum desirable. There is more potential out there than in Amarillo, and the penetration is less. But this area is even more remote and difficult to work from Dallas, in spite of the fact that many factory representatives do work it from there. No more than eighty should be considered because there must be other volume closer to home that should be easier and less expensive to obtain.

In order to make the most of the allocated time in the area, it would be sensible to fly to El Paso or Albuquerque, rent a car, work the territory, and save the two or more days of driving out there and back. At some future date, an increased market share might become important enough to justify a review of this allocation.

LUBBOCK—100 Calls

It appears reasonable to consider Lubbock next. The specification of ninety-two calls should be boosted to 100 to provide five trips of one week each for the year. This is the third most important sector, and the quota calls for a 15 percent increase for the next year. In the near future, this area should become even more important to us, and we hope it will justify several more trips per year. In the meantime, if there is any surplus time this year, it would be easy to run to Amarillo on any Lubbock trip.

OKLAHOMA—140 Calls

For the theoretical 148 calls due Oklahoma, 140 seems a good amount. This will provide seven trips for the year, and that should be ample to gain a modest 8.8 percent increase. The 140 calls should give time for more increase than that and a bigger share of that market.

EAST TEXAS—44 Calls

and

WACO—24 Calls

East Texas and Waco are really no problem since they are close to Dallas. Any amount of time in full days may be allocated. If more time is needed for a reason more important than a day's work in Dallas/Fort Worth, that time may be taken easily. In both of these areas, there are established customers who do not normally require too much time.

DALLAS/FORT WORTH—252 Calls

That leaves 252 calls for the Dallas/Fort Worth sector. It almost seems that the most important area was held for last to be allocated what remained. That is not so. The area with the largest number of calls provides the most flexibility, but if more calls were needed, changes could be very easily made. The fact is that 252 calls seems an adequate number since there are other factors that work to our benefit in this area. With a regional office and warehouse here, branch personnel are in nearly daily contact with all of our customers. Special service is available to them on a continuing basis, and this contact also affords our people an opportunity to ensure that all of our customers are satisfied or that we know when any problems exist. Our local presence also enhances the value of our line in this local area. Some of our oldest customers are in this locality, and they need less help than some of the newer converts. Even 252 calls, though less than the theoretical share, should be ample to enable us to maintain close contact with all of the important accounts. In effect, we will be spending more than a third of our time in this area, even at the reduced figure. Any problems may be easily given the additional time necessary.

The worksheet completed for this sector totals thus far is shown in Figure B-3.

Study your figures in column 11 and make sure that they reflect the allocation of calls you think is best at the time. If you have further slight adjustments to make, they will be easier to accomplish now than after you complete the other worksheets (one for each sector). Be sure that the number of calls in column 11 totals the same as the number you have estimated for the year, or the number of dollars of sales per call will be distorted from what you have calculated necessary to reach your quota.

You have now allocated your calls by sector for the year on the basis of what appears to best satisfy all of the needs you can envision. Naturally, the numbers might not hold all year in all cases; unforeseen developments might make changes necessary. Whenever this is the case, however, you will benefit from reviewing this original plan. The figures you have shown in the first eleven columns will be relevant unless some change in sales volume results that is radically different from your original quota.

These figures provide an excellent start for your final plan. You

Work Sheet For Planning Territory Coverage

Sector: All Sectors Quota: 1,800,000 Year 1982

COLUMN WRITE	No	Sector	Location	Prod. Class	Estimated Potential	Sales Last Year	Per Cent Penetration	Quota Next Year	Inc. Over Last Year	Calls Theo	Calls Sched	Weeks Theo	Weeks Sched
	1	Dallas/Fort Worth			4000000	600000	15.0%	710000	18.3%	234	252		
	2	East Texas			750000	110000	14.7%	120000	9.1%	48	44		
	3	Waco			150000	36000	24.0%	40000	11.1%	16	24		
	4	Lubbock			1500000	200000	13.3%	230000	15.0%	92	100		
	5	Amarillo			800000	145000	18.1%	170000	17.2%	68	80		
	6	Oklahoma			1800000	340000	18.9%	370000	8.8%	143	140		
	7	El Paso/New Mexico			1200000	150000	12.5%	160000	6.7%	64	80		
		Totals			10200000	1571000	15.5%	1800000	13.9%	720	720		

FIGURE B-3. Worksheet for planning territory coverage—complete through column 11.

know, for example, that Dallas/Fort Worth is entitled to 252 calls for the year, East Texas gets forty-four, Waco merits twenty-four, and so on. These numbers represent a ratio only and, theoretically, that ratio would be properly maintained if you spent the next 252 calls in Dallas/Fort Worth, the next forty-four in East Texas, and on through the other sectors.

But that would be ridiculous, and therein lies the next requirement. You need to determine a schedule that will maintain the ratio of time that you have gone to great effort to determine, and yet will provide regular, periodic attention to all customers and prospects in all sectors. In other words, you must establish a pattern for your sales trips into each sector, and you must do this intelligently or you will nullify much of the painstaking work you have accomplished.

There is a fairly simple way to make the transition that is now required. Determine a cycle and think of a cycle as the shortest period necessary to permit you to cover each sector at least once while you still hold to the ratio of calls each customer merits. This determination will be simplified if you think briefly in terms of weeks rather than calls. And recall that the remote sectors have to be given a full week to make the trip practical. Assume that Amarillo is given a week. What then would be the ratio of time in weeks for the other sectors? The figure for Amarillo in column 11 is 80, indicating eighty calls for the year. Now, if that figure were divided by 80, the result would be 1. That suggests the simple arithmetic to complete column 12.

Column 12—Weeks/Theo.

Divide all figures in column 11 by 80. Assume that the *1* for Amarillo is one week, and when all of the other sectors are also divided by 80, the established ratio of time originally allocated is maintained. And the resultant figures show how many weeks each sector must be given when Amarillo is given one. This is merely a simple arithmetic technique.

Column 13—Weeks/Sched.

Some of the results in column 12 are still not going to be practical. For example, one and one-fourth weeks for Lubbock, and one and three-fourths weeks for Oklahoma would present problems. Each sector, except those close to your home, requires full weeks for any trips into them. The full week increment is accomplished in what seems to be a reasonable rounding-off in column 13, and a cycle of nine weeks is the result. Nine weeks makes a good cycle in that it will make it possible to cover all of the territory at least four times a year in the thirty-six work weeks scheduled.

The result will come into sharper focus in a brief summary:

Sector	Weeks Allocated per Cycle
Dallas/Forth Worth	3
East Texas & Waco (combined)	1
Lubbock	1
Amarillo	1
Oklahoma	2
El Paso/New Mexico	1

This worksheet completed for the sectors in total is shown in Figure B-4.

At this point, you have a pretty good general idea of where you should spend your time. If you follow the suggestion that has developed, you will be devoting your time in about the same ratio as the return you might expect. It has become clear to you by now that only five weeks out of nine will require your travel away from home for the full week. That is not bad for covering a district with so much geography; it should facilitate your finding time in the office for continuing planning, and it should be welcome news for your family.

The worksheet was originally designed to aid in your analysis of every individual customer and prospect, and the proportionate time deserved by each. The sector totals would have resulted automatically if every account had been listed and all line information developed for each one. It seemed advisable, however, to analyze the sectors first. That is the way a quota is determined—the final figure is assigned and then the breakdown into what is involved for each specific account follows from that. As another advantage, the sector totals give a perspective early that is very helpful.

As a matter of fact, this perspective might be in sufficient detail for you for some sectors. For the smaller ones in which you have allocated the minimum four weeks per year, there might be no big problem for you to decide just how to spend that time. If there is, or if you desire more detail for any of the sectors, there is only one more step to complete all details of your planning. The same worksheet will adapt to an analysis of each sector, and the instructions already given should be ample. Use one sheet

Sector __All Sectors__ Worksheet for Planning Territory Coverage Year __1982__

1 No.	2 Sector	3 Location	4 Acct. Class	5 Estimated Potential	6 Sales Last Year	7 Per cent Penetration	8 Quota Next Year	9 Inc. Over Last Year	10 Calls Theo.	Sched.	12 Weeks Theo.	13 Sched.
1	Dallas/Fort Worth			4000000	600000	15.0%	710000	17.5%	274	252	3.5	3
2	East Texas			750000	110000	14.7%	120000	9.1%	48	44	.55	
3	Waco			150000	36000	24.0%	40000	11.1%	116	24	.30	
4	Lubbock			1500000	200000	13.3%	230000	15.0%	92	100	1.25	1
5	Amarillo			800000	145000	18.1%	170000	17.2%	63	80	1.0	1
6	Oklahoma			1800000	340000	18.9%	370000	8.8%	147	140	1.75	2
7	El Paso/New Mexico			1200000	150000	12.5%	160000	6.7%	64	80	1.0	1
	Totals			10200000	1591000	15.5%	1800000	13.9%	720	720	9.00	9

FIGURE B-4. Worksheet for planning territory coverage—complete through column 12.

for each sector, for ease of handling and reference. Note that columns 12 and 13 are not applicable.

In completing the sheets for each sector, list the active accounts first by location, show a miscellaneous group after that, and list the prospects last. The miscellaneous group should include the smaller, erratic purchasers who really do not merit any significant time according to their purchases, but who are legitimate customers you do not want to purge from your list. They are legitimate in that they qualify for a trade classification and are buying at the price for that classification. In addition, there is a remote chance that some day they will be buying enough to qualify for more direct attention from you. If that does not happen, you might later suggest that they buy from one of your distributors, who will be able to serve their limited needs more efficiently than you will.

Be as specific as you can about prospects. Show the name and location of each if you know who they are. If not, show "Prospect" for an indication that one is to be determined, and show the city in which it is needed or possibly available. Complete the rest of the columns so far as possible for each prospect. Naturally you will show a city or trade center where you have at least some idea that one is available or will become available because of the growth of the area, the development of the industry prominent in the area, or some other indication that there will be more business there for you. Show an estimate of the volume you expect if available. You will definitely need to specify the volume estimate if that amount is to be included in the quota you have been assigned, but in that case, be realistic. If you expect to close a prospect in a given location that will buy $50,000 per year of your products, do not include the full $50,000 unless you can complete the sale readily. If it will take six months to close the prospect, you must expect only $25,000 during the first year.

All sectors may be completed in this manner to give you the maximum detail about your entire district. If you run out of time during your first session, finish the sectors you plan to visit first, and finish the others before your first trip in that direction.

As an example, the Lubbock sector has been analyzed, and the worksheet is shown in Figure B-5. A few explanatory notes might help you:

1. As you will note, details have been completed through column 11, including the allocation of calls to each customer. As noted before, columns 12 and 13 do not apply.

2. Twenty-eight calls for ABC Supply in Lubbock will undoubtedly

Sector — LUBBOCK   Worksheet for Planning Territory Coverage   Year 1982

Quota 230,000

No.	Customer or Prospect	Location	Acct. Class	Estimated Potential	Sales Last Year	Per Cent Penetration	Quota Next Year	Inc. over Last Year	Calls Theor.	Calls Sched.	Weeks Theor.	Weeks Sched.
1												
2	ABC Supply	LUBBOCK	D	100000	60000	60.0%	68000	13.3%	27.2	27		
3	Farm Harvester	LUBBOCK	O	30000	20000	66.6%	23000	15.0%	9.2	4		
4												
5	Western MFG Co.	ABILENE	O	60000	30000	50.0%	53000	10.0%	13.2	6		
6												
7	Oil Field Supply	ODESSA	D	100000	30000	30.0%	50000	0	12.0	10		
8	Ector Distributor	ODESSA	D	25000	20000	80.0%	22000	10.0%	8.8	8		
9												
10	Big State Cement	MIDLAND	C	40000	25000	62.5%	25000	0.0%	10.0	4		
11												
12	Miscellaneous			20000	15000	75.0%	17000	13.5%	6.8	5		
13												
14	Abilene Supply	ABILENE	DP				12000		4.8	6		
15												
16												
17	Prospect	LUBBOCK	DP									
18	Prospect	LUBBOCK	DP									
19	Prospect	SONANGELO	O									
20												
21												
22												
23	Totals				200000		230000		92.0	69		
24												
25												

FIGURE B-5. Worksheet for planning territory coverage—Lubbock Sector.

strike you as being a lot. Bear in mind that this includes any calls to be made with distributor salespersons.

3. The total number of calls does not equal the total provided in four weeks—eighty in all. Any extra calls should be used to spend more time locating new prospects and for calling on competitive distributors. If you are to learn all about what goes on in your district, you will be able to use all of the calls available to you.

4. At this point, you are permitted all of the flexibility you need in using the figures to satisfy particular requirements and changing conditions. The fact that you have developed the figures rather precisely will provide you with good instincts about finally deciding where to spend your time. And there is one other important consideration that becomes a determinant in your allocation of time. You will be following very closely the attainment of the quotas you have assigned to each customer, and if one falls behind, you will devote the extra attention necessary to that account.

The remaining planning necessary to complete your total effort in this respect may be resumed in the basic text on Page 151, PLANNING FOR URBAN TERRITORIES.

Index